NAME:
_____

CLASS:
_____

Children often struggle with math. Of course, math is one of the most common and vast subject that children have difficulty with. However, it can be easier with the adequate effort, training and practice. For those 5th and 6th grade children who require extra practice to be good at math, **the Fast Math Success Workbook Grade 5-6** is the right decision. It provides variety of math topics aligned with common core standards with a lot of math problems.

This book provides sequential topics from foundations to harder topics because children can only understand advanced topics if they have completely grasped the basic concepts. For example, to solve an algebra or a fraction problem, children must know the basic addition, subtraction, multiplication, division and numeration.

Therefore, the best way to master math is to practice regularly and learn from the mistakes. This book provides practice worksheets on important math topics carefully selected for children to help advance in math. After completing this book, children will be able to recognize, understand, provide solution to a math problem. Moreover, this book will also build confidence for school tests and exams which are often unknown and create trouble for children.

We have provided solutions to all the practice problem given in the book; therefore, if you feel difficulty, just go to back of the book, locate the answer, and try to understand why this is the right answer and what you must do to come up with that solution. And once you understand the mistake, master the correct steps to solve the problem, and never repeat the mistake. **This is the secret way to Fast Math Success.**

This book can be used in classroom for math activity, extra practice, homework, homeschooling, and for teacher companion for non-prep guide.

Contents

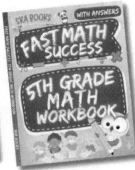

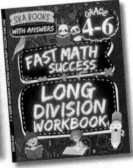

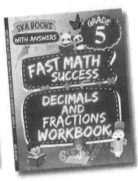

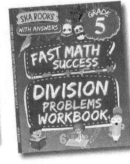

Pre-Algebra - Order of Operations (PEMDAS)

Find the solution.

① $(-67) - 82 + 65 =$ _____

② $93(-57 + 74) =$ _____

③ $(50 + 64) \div 60 =$ _____

④ $39 + (-77) + 49 =$ _____

⑤ $(4 + 55) \times (14 + 49) =$ _____

⑥ $17 + (-48 + 6) =$ _____

⑦ $(67 + 20) \div 74 =$ _____

⑧ $40 + 46 - (49 + 14) =$ _____

⑨ $86(-93 + 86) =$ _____

⑩ $45 + 20 - 6 =$ _____

Pre-Algebra - Order of Operations (PEMDAS)

Find the solution.

① $(74 + 32) \times (92 + 13) = $ _____

⑫ $(93 + 64)(44 + 33) = $ _____

⑬ $26 \times 70 = $ _____

⑭ $42 + 29 + 58 + 93 = $ _____

⑮ $(43 + 20)(45 + 44) = $ _____

⑯ $88 \times (57 + 78) = $ _____

⑰ $15(20 + 72) = $ _____

⑱ $(31^1) \times (63^1) + 84 = $ _____

⑲ $85 - 74 - (-22) = $ _____

⑳ $8 + 82 - (66 + 22) = $ _____

Pre-Algebra - Order of Operations (PEMDAS)

Find the solution.

21. $64 + (89 \times 82) =$ _____

22. $76 - (-85) - (-56) =$ _____

23. $50 - (-97) - 36 =$ _____

24. $(44 + 20)^1 + (59 + 13)^1 =$ _____

25. $21 \times 81 =$ _____

26. $30 + 79^1 + 59 + 59^1 =$ _____

27. $(4 + 63)60 - 62 =$ _____

28. $(-36) + (-94) + 36 =$ _____

29. $67 \times 8 =$ _____

30. $(24 + 66)9 - 24 =$ _____

Pre-Algebra - Order of Operations (PEMDAS)

Find the solution.

(31) $46 \times (23 + 3) =$ _____

(32) $40 + 95^1 =$ _____

(33) $32 + (-55) + 90 =$ _____

(34) $43 + (-90 + 95) =$ _____

(35) $16 \times (86 + 5) =$ _____

(36) $27 + (-46) - 82 =$ _____

(37) $50 + (-89 + 43) =$ _____

(38) $(74 + 70) \times (36 + 95) =$ _____

(39) $(64 + 42)^1 =$ _____

(40) $13 + 39 - (-49) =$ _____

Pre-Algebra - Order of Operations (PEMDAS)

Find the solution.

41 $35 \times 52 =$ _____

42 $34 + 23 + 18 =$ _____

43 $(29 + 79) \div 84 =$ _____

44 $4 + 15 + 36 =$ _____

45 $(27^1) \times (51^1) + 29 =$ _____

46 $(-29) + (-37) + 76 =$ _____

47 $(87 + 7) \times (76 + 53) =$ _____

48 $19 + 17 + 42 + 72 =$ _____

49 $(32^1) \times (54^1) + 83 =$ _____

50 $(33 + 90) \times (87 + 12) =$ _____

Name:
_____

Date:
__/__/____

Time Taken:
_____ Min

Pre-Algebra - Order of Operations (PEMDAS)

Find the solution.

(51) $(-9) - 24 + 14 =$ _____

(52) $44 - 8 - (-13) =$ _____

(53) $(4 + 17)(38 + 52) =$ _____

(54) $28 \times (78 + 87) =$ _____

(55) $(17 + 36) \times (92 + 51) =$ _____

(56) $(86 + 74)^1 =$ _____

(57) $95 + (-51) + (-14) =$ _____

(58) $(28 + 24) \div 98 =$ _____

(59) $42 + (-74 + 39) =$ _____

(60) $96 + 30 - 70 =$ _____

Pre-Algebra - Order of Operations (PEMDAS)

Find the solution.

(61) $17 \times (53 + 35) =$ _____

(62) $84 \times (50 + 22) =$ _____

(63) $38 + 54 - (48 + 95) =$ _____

(64) $(-31) - 92 - 89 =$ _____

(65) $(7 + 95)(96 - 89) =$ _____

(66) $(-45) - 66 + 38 =$ _____

(67) $(-65) - 21 + 8 =$ _____

(68) $82 + (-88) - 87 =$ _____

(69) $(91 + 7) \div 44 =$ _____

(70) $(64^1) \times (22^1) + 63 =$ _____

Pre-Algebra - Order of Operations (PEMDAS)

Find the solution.

71 $48 + 34 + 39 =$ _____

72 $(-46) + 1 - (-89) =$ _____

73 $15 + 95 + 39 + 83 =$ _____

74 $57 + 4 + 15 + 96 =$ _____

75 $45(-53 + 96) =$ _____

76 $62 \times (30 + 32) =$ _____

77 $(10 + 84)^1 + (74 + 68)^1 =$ _____

78 $60 - (-74) - (-72) =$ _____

79 $35 + 5 - 50 + 95 =$ _____

80 $46 + (-2 + 80) =$ _____

Name: _____

Date: __/__/____

Time Taken: ___ Min

Fractions Addition - Unlike Denominator

Find the sum.

(81) $\dfrac{32}{36} + \dfrac{10}{11} =$ _____

(82) $\dfrac{18}{19} + \dfrac{8}{36} =$ _____

(83) $\dfrac{4}{10} + \dfrac{1}{3} =$ _____

(84) $\dfrac{20}{25} + \dfrac{5}{11} =$ _____

(85) $\dfrac{7}{18} + \dfrac{3}{7} =$ _____

(86) $\dfrac{47}{100} + \dfrac{10}{16} =$ _____

(87) $\dfrac{1}{2} + \dfrac{35}{40} =$ _____

(88) $\dfrac{10}{16} + \dfrac{60}{75} =$ _____

(89) $\dfrac{23}{36} + \dfrac{3}{5} =$ _____

(90) $\dfrac{12}{32} + \dfrac{2}{23} =$ _____

Fractions Addition - Unlike Denominator

Find the sum.

(91) $\dfrac{17}{30} + \dfrac{4}{12} =$ _____

(92) $\dfrac{2}{14} + \dfrac{1}{4} =$ _____

(93) $\dfrac{2}{5} + \dfrac{14}{19} =$ _____

(94) $\dfrac{1}{2} + \dfrac{5}{7} =$ _____

(95) $\dfrac{14}{18} + \dfrac{3}{6} =$ _____

(96) $\dfrac{64}{70} + \dfrac{3}{8} =$ _____

(97) $\dfrac{2}{10} + \dfrac{39}{60} =$ _____

(98) $\dfrac{4}{25} + \dfrac{16}{25} =$ _____

(99) $\dfrac{11}{16} + \dfrac{3}{4} =$ _____

(100) $\dfrac{5}{40} + \dfrac{18}{22} =$ _____

Fractions Addition - Unlike Denominator

Find the sum.

(101) $\dfrac{2}{4} + \dfrac{12}{16} =$ _____

(102) $\dfrac{21}{22} + \dfrac{9}{100} =$ _____

(103) $\dfrac{20}{50} + \dfrac{15}{20} =$ _____

(104) $\dfrac{15}{21} + \dfrac{9}{13} =$ _____

(105) $\dfrac{2}{14} + \dfrac{8}{24} =$ _____

(106) $\dfrac{33}{40} + \dfrac{5}{7} =$ _____

(107) $\dfrac{2}{10} + \dfrac{7}{8} =$ _____

(108) $\dfrac{15}{32} + \dfrac{6}{23} =$ _____

(109) $\dfrac{2}{50} + \dfrac{17}{24} =$ _____

(110) $\dfrac{15}{16} + \dfrac{11}{14} =$ _____

Name: _____

Date: __/__/____

Time Taken: ___ Min

Fractions Addition - Unlike Denominator

Find the sum.

(111) $\dfrac{3}{10} + \dfrac{7}{13} =$ _____

(112) $\dfrac{6}{25} + \dfrac{3}{6} =$ _____

(113) $\dfrac{10}{17} + \dfrac{6}{15} =$ _____

(114) $\dfrac{17}{24} + \dfrac{8}{19} =$ _____

(115) $\dfrac{11}{13} + \dfrac{36}{40} =$ _____

(116) $\dfrac{36}{50} + \dfrac{15}{30} =$ _____

(117) $\dfrac{29}{30} + \dfrac{20}{22} =$ _____

(118) $\dfrac{1}{2} + \dfrac{1}{2} =$ _____

(119) $\dfrac{5}{6} + \dfrac{31}{36} =$ _____

(120) $\dfrac{61}{75} + \dfrac{62}{100} =$ _____

Fractions Addition - Unlike Denominator

Find the sum.

(121) $\dfrac{3}{7} + \dfrac{2}{12} =$ _____

(122) $\dfrac{5}{19} + \dfrac{3}{30} =$ _____

(123) $\dfrac{14}{22} + \dfrac{11}{15} =$ _____

(124) $\dfrac{6}{14} + \dfrac{3}{4} =$ _____

(125) $\dfrac{6}{15} + \dfrac{3}{9} =$ _____

(126) $\dfrac{39}{50} + \dfrac{28}{30} =$ _____

(127) $\dfrac{18}{24} + \dfrac{9}{16} =$ _____

(128) $\dfrac{4}{6} + \dfrac{10}{60} =$ _____

(129) $\dfrac{2}{3} + \dfrac{2}{4} =$ _____

(130) $\dfrac{16}{32} + \dfrac{35}{36} =$ _____

Fractions Subtraction - Unlike Denominator

Find the difference.

(131) $\dfrac{15}{19} - \dfrac{3}{14} =$ _____

(132) $\dfrac{9}{16} - \dfrac{17}{50} =$ _____

(133) $\dfrac{1}{2} - \dfrac{1}{3} =$ _____

(134) $\dfrac{11}{17} - \dfrac{8}{21} =$ _____

(135) $\dfrac{25}{75} - \dfrac{2}{10} =$ _____

(136) $\dfrac{6}{7} - \dfrac{1}{2} =$ _____

(137) $\dfrac{8}{18} - \dfrac{2}{9} =$ _____

(138) $\dfrac{3}{13} - \dfrac{3}{22} =$ _____

(139) $\dfrac{14}{15} - \dfrac{8}{11} =$ _____

(140) $\dfrac{3}{4} - \dfrac{11}{20} =$ _____

Fractions Subtraction - Unlike Denominator

Find the difference.

(141) $\frac{55}{75} - \frac{4}{10} =$ _____

(142) $\frac{2}{13} - \frac{2}{22} =$ _____

(143) $\frac{14}{25} - \frac{8}{16} =$ _____

(144) $\frac{9}{16} - \frac{3}{36} =$ _____

(145) $\frac{6}{19} - \frac{3}{40} =$ _____

(146) $\frac{4}{8} - \frac{7}{21} =$ _____

(147) $\frac{1}{4} - \frac{2}{19} =$ _____

(148) $\frac{18}{20} - \frac{14}{32} =$ _____

(149) $\frac{7}{22} - \frac{17}{70} =$ _____

(150) $\frac{2}{3} - \frac{7}{25} =$ _____

Fractions Subtraction - Unlike Denominator

Find the difference.

(151) $\dfrac{3}{4} - \dfrac{7}{10} =$ _____

(152) $\dfrac{5}{6} - \dfrac{1}{6} =$ _____

(153) $\dfrac{2}{8} - \dfrac{1}{5} =$ _____

(154) $\dfrac{2}{3} - \dfrac{2}{8} =$ _____

(155) $\dfrac{6}{12} - \dfrac{1}{3} =$ _____

(156) $\dfrac{3}{5} - \dfrac{1}{5} =$ _____

(157) $\dfrac{4}{6} - \dfrac{5}{8} =$ _____

(158) $\dfrac{2}{5} - \dfrac{1}{6} =$ _____

(159) $\dfrac{5}{10} - \dfrac{1}{4} =$ _____

(160) $\dfrac{8}{12} - \dfrac{1}{5} =$ _____

Fractions Subtraction - Unlike Denominator

Find the difference.

(161) $\dfrac{58}{75} - \dfrac{1}{12} =$ _____

(162) $\dfrac{12}{16} - \dfrac{2}{6} =$ _____

(163) $\dfrac{18}{22} - \dfrac{2}{8} =$ _____

(164) $\dfrac{17}{25} - \dfrac{2}{5} =$ _____

(165) $\dfrac{2}{11} - \dfrac{6}{50} =$ _____

(166) $\dfrac{10}{12} - \dfrac{16}{23} =$ _____

(167) $\dfrac{30}{36} - \dfrac{2}{6} =$ _____

(168) $\dfrac{58}{75} - \dfrac{3}{30} =$ _____

(169) $\dfrac{8}{9} - \dfrac{14}{20} =$ _____

(170) $\dfrac{16}{19} - \dfrac{1}{14} =$ _____

Name:

Date:
___/___/___

Time Taken:
_____ Min

Fractions Subtraction - Unlike Denominator

Find the difference.

(171) $\dfrac{70}{100} - \dfrac{2}{3} =$ _____

(172) $\dfrac{8}{11} - \dfrac{7}{16} =$ _____

(173) $\dfrac{7}{10} - \dfrac{14}{22} =$ _____

(174) $\dfrac{23}{24} - \dfrac{3}{7} =$ _____

(175) $\dfrac{25}{50} - \dfrac{18}{60} =$ _____

(176) $\dfrac{7}{22} - \dfrac{23}{100} =$ _____

(177) $\dfrac{9}{15} - \dfrac{1}{3} =$ _____

(178) $\dfrac{34}{75} - \dfrac{3}{17} =$ _____

(179) $\dfrac{1}{3} - \dfrac{1}{5} =$ _____

(180) $\dfrac{5}{6} - \dfrac{4}{10} =$ _____

Fractions Multiplication

Find the product.

(181) $\dfrac{7}{11} \times \dfrac{14}{18} =$ _____

(182) $\dfrac{1}{2} \times \dfrac{7}{9} =$ _____

(183) $\dfrac{50}{60} \times \dfrac{2}{24} =$ _____

(184) $\dfrac{13}{15} \times \dfrac{4}{22} =$ _____

(185) $\dfrac{30}{40} \times \dfrac{2}{5} =$ _____

(186) $\dfrac{10}{14} \times \dfrac{28}{50} =$ _____

(187) $\dfrac{1}{8} \times \dfrac{4}{13} =$ _____

(188) $\dfrac{17}{18} \times \dfrac{14}{25} =$ _____

(189) $\dfrac{4}{9} \times \dfrac{14}{21} =$ _____

(190) $\dfrac{5}{6} \times \dfrac{2}{19} =$ _____

(191) $\dfrac{7}{32} \times \dfrac{8}{20} =$ _____

(192) $\dfrac{2}{3} \times \dfrac{18}{24} =$ _____

(193) $\dfrac{5}{30} \times \dfrac{3}{4} =$ _____

(194) $\dfrac{57}{70} \times \dfrac{38}{40} =$ _____

(195) $\dfrac{19}{25} \times \dfrac{13}{16} =$ _____

(196) $\dfrac{5}{8} \times \dfrac{4}{12} =$ _____

(197) $\dfrac{14}{21} \times \dfrac{7}{11} =$ _____

(198) $\dfrac{7}{11} \times \dfrac{7}{13} =$ _____

(199) $\dfrac{75}{100} \times \dfrac{3}{9} =$ _____

(200) $\dfrac{2}{5} \times \dfrac{57}{70} =$ _____

Fractions Multiplication

Find the product.

(201) $\frac{25}{30} \times \frac{10}{16} =$ _____

(202) $\frac{34}{60} \times \frac{41}{100} =$ _____

(203) $\frac{7}{19} \times \frac{2}{5} =$ _____

(204) $\frac{6}{10} \times \frac{3}{6} =$ _____

(205) $\frac{1}{2} \times \frac{28}{60} =$ _____

(206) $\frac{3}{13} \times \frac{13}{22} =$ _____

(207) $\frac{7}{32} \times \frac{18}{23} =$ _____

(208) $\frac{6}{8} \times \frac{7}{25} =$ _____

(209) $\frac{2}{7} \times \frac{4}{100} =$ _____

(210) $\frac{11}{18} \times \frac{1}{2} =$ _____

(211) $\frac{5}{21} \times \frac{29}{32} =$ _____

(212) $\frac{6}{15} \times \frac{22}{24} =$ _____

(213) $\frac{72}{100} \times \frac{24}{60} =$ _____

(214) $\frac{5}{6} \times \frac{32}{70} =$ _____

(215) $\frac{15}{24} \times \frac{5}{11} =$ _____

(216) $\frac{33}{40} \times \frac{3}{18} =$ _____

(217) $\frac{12}{30} \times \frac{1}{5} =$ _____

(218) $\frac{3}{13} \times \frac{2}{4} =$ _____

(219) $\frac{18}{22} \times \frac{3}{16} =$ _____

(220) $\frac{4}{10} \times \frac{11}{15} =$ _____

Fractions Multiplication

Find the product.

(221) $\frac{3}{7} \times \frac{14}{36} =$ _____

(222) $\frac{2}{10} \times \frac{7}{20} =$ _____

(223) $\frac{49}{75} \times \frac{1}{12} =$ _____

(224) $\frac{3}{21} \times \frac{14}{17} =$ _____

(225) $\frac{58}{70} \times \frac{3}{8} =$ _____

(226) $\frac{2}{4} \times \frac{36}{50} =$ _____

(227) $\frac{17}{24} \times \frac{3}{7} =$ _____

(228) $\frac{13}{22} \times \frac{33}{36} =$ _____

(229) $\frac{6}{20} \times \frac{38}{60} =$ _____

(230) $\frac{41}{60} \times \frac{67}{70} =$ _____

(231) $\frac{12}{23} \times \frac{2}{20} =$ _____

(232) $\frac{20}{25} \times \frac{44}{100} =$ _____

(233) $\frac{12}{19} \times \frac{1}{6} =$ _____

(234) $\frac{7}{36} \times \frac{2}{25} =$ _____

(235) $\frac{6}{10} \times \frac{11}{40} =$ _____

(236) $\frac{16}{40} \times \frac{1}{10} =$ _____

(237) $\frac{2}{3} \times \frac{8}{9} =$ _____

(238) $\frac{4}{8} \times \frac{18}{22} =$ _____

(239) $\frac{4}{5} \times \frac{2}{24} =$ _____

(240) $\frac{6}{21} \times \frac{7}{11} =$ _____

Fractions Division

Find the quotient.

(241) $\dfrac{6}{21} \div \dfrac{1}{16} =$ _____

(242) $\dfrac{15}{25} \div \dfrac{3}{11} =$ _____

(243) $\dfrac{3}{32} \div \dfrac{7}{60} =$ _____

(244) $\dfrac{4}{8} \div \dfrac{1}{20} =$ _____

(245) $\dfrac{6}{10} \div \dfrac{7}{22} =$ _____

(246) $\dfrac{20}{70} \div \dfrac{4}{17} =$ _____

(247) $\dfrac{3}{7} \div \dfrac{1}{3} =$ _____

(248) $\dfrac{3}{13} \div \dfrac{8}{32} =$ _____

(249) $\dfrac{59}{100} \div \dfrac{1}{2} =$ _____

(250) $\dfrac{11}{16} \div \dfrac{19}{30} =$ _____

Fractions Division

Find the quotient.

(251) $\dfrac{20}{23} \div \dfrac{3}{30} =$ _____

(252) $\dfrac{9}{30} \div \dfrac{14}{25} =$ _____

(253) $\dfrac{1}{14} \div \dfrac{2}{7} =$ _____

(254) $\dfrac{1}{13} \div \dfrac{13}{17} =$ _____

(255) $\dfrac{2}{3} \div \dfrac{9}{12} =$ _____

(256) $\dfrac{2}{10} \div \dfrac{4}{19} =$ _____

(257) $\dfrac{9}{24} \div \dfrac{1}{30} =$ _____

(258) $\dfrac{9}{14} \div \dfrac{25}{50} =$ _____

(259) $\dfrac{3}{7} \div \dfrac{42}{75} =$ _____

(260) $\dfrac{9}{23} \div \dfrac{31}{60} =$ _____

Fractions Division

Find the quotient.

(261) $\dfrac{10}{17} \div \dfrac{3}{22} =$ _____

(262) $\dfrac{24}{50} \div \dfrac{7}{24} =$ _____

(263) $\dfrac{17}{18} \div \dfrac{1}{3} =$ _____

(264) $\dfrac{8}{15} \div \dfrac{4}{15} =$ _____

(265) $\dfrac{3}{5} \div \dfrac{15}{50} =$ _____

(266) $\dfrac{2}{7} \div \dfrac{9}{75} =$ _____

(267) $\dfrac{7}{19} \div \dfrac{7}{11} =$ _____

(268) $\dfrac{8}{11} \div \dfrac{3}{14} =$ _____

(269) $\dfrac{17}{24} \div \dfrac{1}{9} =$ _____

(270) $\dfrac{5}{21} \div \dfrac{7}{10} =$ _____

Name: _____

Date: __/__/____

Time Taken: ____ Min

Multiplication with Whole Numbers

Multiply.

(271) $\frac{4}{6}$ of 3 = _____

(272) $1 \times \frac{1}{5} =$ _____

(273) $7 \times \frac{3}{6} =$ _____

(274) $1 \times \frac{4}{5} =$ _____

(275) $\frac{2}{8}$ of 1 = _____

(276) $1 \times \frac{2}{4} =$ _____

(277) $7 \times \frac{2}{3} =$ _____

(278) $5 \times \frac{1}{8} =$ _____

(279) $\frac{1}{3}$ of 8 = _____

(280) $5 \times \frac{2}{6} =$ _____

(281) $4 \times \frac{2}{5} =$ _____

(282) $9 \times \frac{2}{4} =$ _____

(283) $1 \times \frac{2}{3} =$ _____

(284) $1 \times \frac{2}{6} =$ _____

(285) $\frac{1}{8}$ of 5 = _____

(286) $\frac{3}{4}$ of 2 = _____

(287) $6 \times \frac{1}{5} =$ _____

(288) $4 \times \frac{3}{6} =$ _____

(289) $\frac{2}{8}$ of 6 = _____

(290) $2 \times \frac{1}{3} =$ _____

Fast Math Success Workbook Grade 5-6

Multiplication with Whole Numbers

Multiply.

(291) $\frac{1}{4}$ of 3 = _____

(292) $\frac{7}{8}$ of 4 = _____

(293) $7 \times \frac{3}{4}$ = _____

(294) $\frac{6}{8}$ of 9 = _____

(295) $5 \times \frac{3}{5}$ = _____

(296) $9 \times \frac{1}{3}$ = _____

(297) $2 \times \frac{2}{6}$ = _____

(298) $2 \times \frac{1}{4}$ = _____

(299) $9 \times \frac{1}{3}$ = _____

(300) $3 \times \frac{3}{6}$ = _____

(301) $\frac{1}{5}$ of 3 = _____

(302) $2 \times \frac{5}{8}$ = _____

(303) $2 \times \frac{1}{3}$ = _____

(304) $\frac{3}{6}$ of 1 = _____

(305) $3 \times \frac{4}{8}$ = _____

(306) $8 \times \frac{3}{4}$ = _____

(307) $8 \times \frac{2}{5}$ = _____

(308) $1 \times \frac{4}{6}$ = _____

(309) $1 \times \frac{5}{8}$ = _____

(310) $\frac{2}{5}$ of 8 = _____

Multiplication with Whole Numbers

Multiply.

(311) $\frac{3}{4}$ of 2 = _____

(312) $\frac{2}{3}$ of 6 = _____

(313) $1 \times \frac{1}{6}$ = _____

(314) $7 \times \frac{2}{3}$ = _____

(315) $\frac{1}{5}$ of 6 = _____

(316) $3 \times \frac{2}{8}$ = _____

(317) $\frac{1}{8}$ of 2 = _____

(318) $\frac{3}{4}$ of 5 = _____

(319) $\frac{2}{3}$ of 1 = _____

(320) $\frac{3}{5}$ of 9 = _____

(321) $\frac{4}{6}$ of 7 = _____

(322) $7 \times \frac{1}{4}$ = _____

(323) $7 \times \frac{1}{6}$ = _____

(324) $6 \times \frac{1}{3}$ = _____

(325) $9 \times \frac{4}{5}$ = _____

(326) $\frac{7}{8}$ of 6 = _____

(327) $\frac{1}{6}$ of 1 = _____

(328) $7 \times \frac{2}{8}$ = _____

(329) $\frac{2}{5}$ of 1 = _____

(330) $\frac{1}{4}$ of 1 = _____

Division with Whole Numbers

Divide.

331) $\frac{4}{8} \div 2 =$ _____

332) $\frac{2}{3} \div 1 =$ _____

333) $\frac{5}{6} \div 2 =$ _____

334) $\frac{1}{4} \div 9 =$ _____

335) $\frac{3}{5} \div 3 =$ _____

336) $\frac{3}{5} \div 4 =$ _____

337) $\frac{2}{3} \div 6 =$ _____

338) $\frac{4}{8} \div 9 =$ _____

339) $\frac{1}{6} \div 9 =$ _____

340) $\frac{3}{4} \div 4 =$ _____

341) $\frac{4}{5} \div 5 =$ _____

342) $\frac{2}{3} \div 8 =$ _____

343) $\frac{5}{6} \div 1 =$ _____

344) $\frac{5}{8} \div 3 =$ _____

345) $\frac{3}{4} \div 4 =$ _____

346) $\frac{4}{5} \div 7 =$ _____

347) $\frac{2}{4} \div 2 =$ _____

348) $\frac{3}{8} \div 5 =$ _____

349) $\frac{2}{6} \div 8 =$ _____

350) $\frac{2}{3} \div 7 =$ _____

Division with Whole Numbers

Divide.

(351) $\frac{2}{3} \div 4 =$ _____

(352) $\frac{7}{8} \div 8 =$ _____

(353) $\frac{1}{5} \div 9 =$ _____

(354) $\frac{1}{6} \div 4 =$ _____

(355) $\frac{2}{4} \div 2 =$ _____

(356) $\frac{1}{3} \div 4 =$ _____

(357) $\frac{3}{6} \div 6 =$ _____

(358) $\frac{1}{4} \div 5 =$ _____

(359) $\frac{4}{8} \div 6 =$ _____

(360) $\frac{1}{5} \div 8 =$ _____

(361) $\frac{2}{6} \div 6 =$ _____

(362) $\frac{2}{4} \div 9 =$ _____

(363) $\frac{5}{8} \div 9 =$ _____

(364) $\frac{1}{5} \div 4 =$ _____

(365) $\frac{2}{3} \div 3 =$ _____

(366) $\frac{3}{5} \div 7 =$ _____

(367) $\frac{6}{8} \div 3 =$ _____

(368) $\frac{3}{4} \div 4 =$ _____

(369) $\frac{5}{6} \div 1 =$ _____

(370) $\frac{1}{3} \div 6 =$ _____

Division with Whole Numbers

Divide.

371) $\dfrac{2}{8} \div 6 =$ _____

372) $\dfrac{2}{3} \div 5 =$ _____

373) $\dfrac{2}{4} \div 3 =$ _____

374) $\dfrac{3}{5} \div 2 =$ _____

375) $\dfrac{1}{5} \div 9 =$ _____

376) $\dfrac{3}{8} \div 7 =$ _____

377) $\dfrac{2}{4} \div 5 =$ _____

378) $\dfrac{1}{6} \div 1 =$ _____

379) $\dfrac{1}{3} \div 9 =$ _____

380) $\dfrac{2}{6} \div 1 =$ _____

381) $\dfrac{1}{3} \div 6 =$ _____

382) $\dfrac{4}{8} \div 8 =$ _____

383) $\dfrac{3}{4} \div 9 =$ _____

384) $\dfrac{4}{5} \div 7 =$ _____

385) $\dfrac{3}{4} \div 2 =$ _____

386) $\dfrac{5}{8} \div 3 =$ _____

387) $\dfrac{4}{5} \div 8 =$ _____

388) $\dfrac{2}{6} \div 6 =$ _____

389) $\dfrac{1}{3} \div 8 =$ _____

390) $\dfrac{1}{4} \div 2 =$ _____

Mixed Fractions - Multiplication

Calculate.

(391) $4\frac{7}{60} \times 7\frac{3}{36} =$ _____

(392) $8\frac{4}{19} \times 3\frac{15}{21} =$ _____

(393) $7\frac{5}{8} \times 3\frac{12}{16} =$ _____

(394) $9\frac{4}{11} \times 3\frac{2}{9} =$ _____

(395) $4\frac{13}{15} \times 9\frac{1}{2} =$ _____

(396) $9\frac{11}{22} \times 4\frac{2}{17} =$ _____

(397) $9\frac{3}{6} \times 1\frac{8}{14} =$ _____

(398) $9\frac{7}{32} \times 7\frac{65}{75} =$ _____

(399) $1\frac{36}{40} \times 8\frac{14}{15} =$ _____

(400) $2\frac{19}{25} \times 7\frac{6}{9} =$ _____

Mixed Fractions - Multiplication

Calculate.

(401) $5\frac{5}{36} \times 9\frac{64}{75} =$ _____

(402) $2\frac{7}{9} \times 5\frac{6}{11} =$ _____

(403) $5\frac{13}{15} \times 4\frac{6}{7} =$ _____

(404) $3\frac{1}{4} \times 6\frac{3}{60} =$ _____

(405) $2\frac{4}{24} \times 1\frac{16}{23} =$ _____

(406) $7\frac{12}{17} \times 6\frac{13}{14} =$ _____

(407) $1\frac{1}{2} \times 8\frac{2}{10} =$ _____

(408) $4\frac{1}{8} \times 4\frac{14}{19} =$ _____

(409) $2\frac{1}{3} \times 2\frac{17}{18} =$ _____

(410) $3\frac{19}{22} \times 6\frac{37}{100} =$ _____

Mixed Fractions - Multiplication

Calculate.

(411) $3\frac{3}{19} \times 1\frac{1}{2} =$ _____

(412) $8\frac{45}{70} \times 3\frac{35}{75} =$ _____

(413) $5\frac{5}{7} \times 8\frac{5}{30} =$ _____

(414) $6\frac{19}{20} \times 1\frac{35}{36} =$ _____

(415) $3\frac{11}{14} \times 2\frac{3}{8} =$ _____

(416) $9\frac{2}{10} \times 6\frac{1}{19} =$ _____

(417) $3\frac{12}{17} \times 2\frac{3}{75} =$ _____

(418) $6\frac{12}{15} \times 4\frac{6}{11} =$ _____

(419) $2\frac{11}{30} \times 8\frac{27}{40} =$ _____

(420) $4\frac{1}{5} \times 1\frac{6}{8} =$ _____

Mixed Fractions- Division

Calculate.

(421) $2\frac{3}{5} \div 2\frac{6}{11} =$ _____

(422) $7\frac{1}{7} \div 8\frac{3}{21} =$ _____

(423) $3\frac{51}{70} \div 1\frac{1}{20} =$ _____

(424) $8\frac{6}{13} \div 5\frac{67}{100} =$ _____

(425) $9\frac{1}{4} \div 1\frac{2}{3} =$ _____

(426) $6\frac{16}{18} \div 6\frac{4}{32} =$ _____

(427) $1\frac{1}{22} \div 2\frac{18}{24} =$ _____

(428) $7\frac{14}{25} \div 3\frac{2}{14} =$ _____

(429) $1\frac{3}{16} \div 1\frac{21}{30} =$ _____

(430) $1\frac{3}{8} \div 6\frac{17}{36} =$ _____

Mixed Fractions- Division

Calculate.

(431) $1\frac{14}{18} \div 6\frac{26}{50} =$ _____

(432) $6\frac{10}{14} \div 7\frac{44}{75} =$ _____

(433) $3\frac{27}{36} \div 7\frac{2}{6} =$ _____

(434) $8\frac{3}{19} \div 5\frac{7}{13} =$ _____

(435) $3\frac{7}{16} \div 5\frac{10}{18} =$ _____

(436) $8\frac{7}{15} \div 4\frac{29}{32} =$ _____

(437) $5\frac{1}{50} \div 6\frac{8}{10} =$ _____

(438) $4\frac{26}{40} \div 7\frac{4}{11} =$ _____

(439) $7\frac{36}{60} \div 8\frac{1}{9} =$ _____

(440) $8\frac{37}{70} \div 4\frac{2}{5} =$ _____

Name:
_____
Date:
__/__/____
Time Taken:
____ Min

Mixed Fractions- Division

Calculate.

(441) $4\frac{43}{100} \div 5\frac{2}{3} =$

(442) $5\frac{16}{50} \div 2\frac{20}{40} =$

(443) $9\frac{11}{24} \div 6\frac{8}{17} =$

(444) $2\frac{2}{4} \div 7\frac{14}{23} =$

(445) $2\frac{2}{30} \div 8\frac{13}{14} =$

(446) $7\frac{7}{32} \div 8\frac{6}{10} =$

(447) $1\frac{12}{21} \div 5\frac{11}{12} =$

(448) $9\frac{9}{13} \div 1\frac{16}{18} =$

(449) $9\frac{1}{8} \div 2\frac{28}{75} =$

(450) $9\frac{8}{21} \div 4\frac{1}{4} =$

Fractions: Multiple Operations

Find the solution.

(451) $(\frac{5}{8} + \frac{3}{8}) \times (\frac{3}{8} + \frac{5}{8}) =$

_____

(452) $(\frac{1}{3} + \frac{2}{3}) \times (\frac{1}{3} + \frac{1}{3}) =$

_____

(453) $\frac{1}{8} + \frac{5}{8} + \frac{1}{8} =$

_____

(454) $(\frac{5}{6} \times \frac{3}{4}) + (\frac{1}{6} \times \frac{1}{4}) =$

_____

(455) $(\frac{1}{3} + \frac{2}{3}) \div \frac{2}{3} =$

_____

(456) $\frac{1}{4} + \frac{3}{4} + \frac{1}{4} =$

_____

(457) $(\frac{1}{6} \times \frac{1}{4}) + (\frac{1}{6} \times \frac{3}{4}) =$

_____

(458) $\frac{2}{3} \times \frac{1}{3} \times \frac{1}{3} =$

_____

(459) $(\frac{4}{5} \times \frac{5}{8}) + (\frac{2}{5} \times \frac{3}{8}) =$

_____

(460) $\frac{7}{8} \times \frac{3}{8} \times \frac{7}{8} =$

_____

Fractions: Multiple Operations

Find the solution.

(461) $(\frac{7}{8} + \frac{7}{8}) - (\frac{1}{4} \times \frac{1}{4}) =$ _____

(462) $\frac{4}{5} \times \frac{1}{5} + \frac{3}{5} =$

_____

(463) $\frac{2}{5} \times \frac{4}{5} \times \frac{3}{5} =$

_____

(464) $\frac{1}{8} + \frac{1}{5} - \frac{1}{8} =$

_____

(465) $(\frac{1}{5} + \frac{2}{5}) - (\frac{1}{4} \times \frac{1}{4}) =$

_____

(466) $\frac{2}{3} \times \frac{1}{3} \times \frac{2}{3} =$

_____

(467) $(\frac{1}{4} + \frac{1}{4}) \times (\frac{1}{4} + \frac{1}{4}) =$

_____

(468) $(\frac{1}{6} \times \frac{1}{4}) + (\frac{5}{6} \times \frac{1}{4}) =$

_____

(469) $\frac{3}{8} \times \frac{1}{3} + \frac{2}{3} =$

_____

(470) $(\frac{4}{5} \times \frac{1}{4}) + (\frac{4}{5} \times \frac{1}{4}) =$

_____

Fractions: Multiple Operations

Find the solution.

(471) $(\frac{2}{3} + \frac{1}{3}) \div \frac{2}{3} =$

_____

(472) $(\frac{1}{6} + \frac{1}{6}) \div \frac{1}{6} =$

_____

(473) $(\frac{1}{5} + \frac{1}{5}) - (\frac{1}{4} \times \frac{1}{4}) =$

_____

(474) $(\frac{3}{5} + \frac{2}{5}) \times (\frac{4}{5} + \frac{2}{5}) =$

_____

(475) $\frac{1}{6} + \frac{2}{3} + \frac{1}{6} + \frac{2}{3} =$

_____

(476) $\frac{2}{5} + \frac{3}{4} + \frac{3}{5} + \frac{1}{4} =$

_____

(477) $\frac{1}{3} + \frac{1}{3} + \frac{1}{3} =$

_____

(478) $\frac{1}{5} + \frac{1}{3} + \frac{1}{5} + \frac{2}{3} =$

_____

(479) $\frac{2}{3} + \frac{1}{4} + \frac{2}{3} + \frac{1}{4} =$

_____

(480) $\frac{7}{8} + \frac{7}{8} + \frac{1}{8} =$

_____

Fractions: Multiple Operations

Find the solution.

(481) $\frac{1}{4} + \frac{1}{6} + \frac{1}{4} + \frac{1}{6} =$

_____

(482) $\frac{7}{8} \times \frac{1}{6} + \frac{5}{6} =$

_____

(483) $(\frac{1}{3} + \frac{2}{3}) \div \frac{1}{3} =$

_____

(484) $\frac{1}{5} + \frac{1}{4} + \frac{2}{5} + \frac{1}{4} =$

_____

(485) $(\frac{1}{8} + \frac{1}{8}) - (\frac{1}{6} \times \frac{1}{6}) =$

_____

(486) $(\frac{3}{5} \times \frac{1}{6}) + (\frac{4}{5} \times \frac{1}{6}) =$

_____

(487) $(\frac{1}{3} + \frac{2}{3}) - (\frac{1}{3} \times \frac{1}{3}) =$

_____

(488) $(\frac{3}{8} \times \frac{7}{8}) + (\frac{3}{8} \times \frac{1}{8}) =$

_____

(489) $\frac{3}{4} + \frac{1}{6} - \frac{1}{4} =$

_____

(490) $\frac{1}{6} + \frac{3}{5} + \frac{1}{6} + \frac{2}{5} =$

_____

Fractions: Multiple Operations

Find the solution.

(491) $\frac{5}{6} \times \frac{4}{5} + \frac{2}{5} =$

_____

(492) $(\frac{1}{4} + \frac{3}{4}) \div \frac{1}{4} =$

_____

(493) $(\frac{1}{8} + \frac{7}{8}) \times (\frac{7}{8} + \frac{5}{8}) =$

_____

(494) $(\frac{4}{5} \times \frac{1}{6}) + (\frac{1}{5} \times \frac{1}{6}) =$

_____

(495) $(\frac{1}{3} + \frac{1}{3}) \div \frac{2}{3} =$

_____

(496) $\frac{1}{3} + \frac{2}{5} + 3 =$

_____

(497) $\frac{5}{6} \times \frac{1}{6} \times \frac{1}{6} =$

_____

(498) $\frac{1}{6} \times \frac{5}{6} \times \frac{1}{6} =$

_____

(499) $(\frac{3}{8} \times \frac{1}{4}) + (\frac{1}{8} \times \frac{1}{4}) =$

_____

(500) $\frac{1}{6} + \frac{5}{6} + 9 =$

_____

Name:

Date:
__/__/____

Time Taken:
____ Min

Fractions: Multiple Operations

Find the solution.

(501) $\frac{5}{8} + \frac{2}{5} + \frac{1}{8} + \frac{2}{5} =$

_____

(502) $\frac{1}{6} + \frac{1}{6} + \frac{1}{6} =$

_____

(503) $(\frac{2}{3} + \frac{2}{3}) \div \frac{1}{3} =$

_____

(504) $\frac{1}{4} + \frac{5}{8} + 6 =$

_____

(505) $\frac{1}{6} + \frac{7}{8} - \frac{1}{6} =$

_____

(506) $\frac{4}{5} + \frac{2}{3} + 8 =$

_____

(507) $(\frac{1}{5} \times \frac{1}{8}) + (\frac{3}{5} \times \frac{5}{8}) =$

_____

(508) $\frac{1}{6} \times \frac{1}{3} + \frac{2}{3} =$

_____

(509) $(\frac{7}{8} + \frac{5}{8}) \times (\frac{5}{8} + \frac{7}{8}) =$

_____

(510) $\frac{3}{8} + \frac{2}{5} - \frac{7}{8} =$

_____

Fractions: Multiple Operations

Find the solution.

(511) $\dfrac{1}{4} + \dfrac{1}{4} - \dfrac{3}{4} =$

_____

(512) $\left(\dfrac{4}{5} + \dfrac{3}{5}\right) \div \dfrac{2}{5} =$

_____

(513) $\dfrac{1}{8} \times \dfrac{1}{8} \times \dfrac{3}{8} =$

_____

(514) $\dfrac{1}{3} \times \dfrac{2}{3} \times \dfrac{1}{3} =$

_____

(515) $\dfrac{1}{8} \times \dfrac{1}{8} \times \dfrac{5}{8} =$

_____

(516) $\left(\dfrac{1}{6} + \dfrac{1}{6}\right) \times \left(\dfrac{1}{6} + \dfrac{5}{6}\right) =$

_____

(517) $\dfrac{1}{3} \times \dfrac{2}{3} + \dfrac{2}{3} =$

_____

(518) $\left(\dfrac{5}{6} + \dfrac{1}{6}\right) - \left(\dfrac{1}{4} \times \dfrac{3}{4}\right) =$

_____

(519) $\left(\dfrac{3}{5} + \dfrac{1}{5}\right) \times \left(\dfrac{2}{5} + \dfrac{1}{5}\right) =$

_____

(520) $\dfrac{3}{5} \times \dfrac{4}{5} \times \dfrac{4}{5} =$

_____

Fractions: Multiple Operations

Find the solution.

(521) $\frac{1}{4} + \frac{1}{5} + \frac{3}{4} + \frac{1}{5} =$

_____

(522) $\frac{5}{8} + \frac{1}{8} + \frac{3}{8} =$

_____

(523) $\frac{3}{4} \times \frac{5}{6} + \frac{1}{6} =$

_____

(524) $\left(\frac{2}{5} + \frac{4}{5}\right) - \left(\frac{3}{5} \times \frac{2}{5}\right) =$

_____

(525) $\frac{3}{8} + \frac{1}{6} + \frac{1}{8} + \frac{1}{6} =$

_____

(526) $\left(\frac{3}{4} + \frac{1}{4}\right) \div \frac{1}{4} =$

_____

(527) $\frac{1}{3} + \frac{3}{5} + \frac{2}{3} + \frac{1}{5} =$

_____

(528) $\left(\frac{3}{5} \times \frac{1}{6}\right) + \left(\frac{3}{5} \times \frac{5}{6}\right) =$

_____

(529) $\left(\frac{5}{6} + \frac{1}{6}\right) \times \left(\frac{1}{6} + \frac{1}{6}\right) =$

_____

(530) $\left(\frac{1}{4} + \frac{1}{4}\right) \times \left(\frac{1}{4} + \frac{1}{4}\right) =$

_____

Fractions: Multiple Operations

Find the solution.

(531) $\frac{5}{8} \times \frac{1}{6} + \frac{1}{6} =$

_____

(532) $\frac{1}{6} + \frac{1}{6} + 8 =$

_____

(533) $(\frac{1}{8} + \frac{5}{8}) - (\frac{2}{3} \times \frac{2}{3}) =$

_____

(534) $(\frac{3}{5} \times \frac{1}{3}) + (\frac{1}{5} \times \frac{1}{3}) =$

_____

(535) $(\frac{4}{5} + \frac{4}{5}) \times (\frac{3}{5} + \frac{4}{5}) =$

_____

(536) $\frac{3}{8} + \frac{5}{8} + \frac{1}{8} + \frac{7}{8} =$

_____

(537) $\frac{1}{6} \times \frac{1}{6} \times \frac{1}{6} =$

_____

(538) $\frac{4}{5} \times \frac{1}{5} \times \frac{3}{5} =$

_____

(539) $(\frac{1}{6} + \frac{1}{6}) \times (\frac{1}{6} + \frac{1}{6}) =$

_____

(540) $\frac{3}{8} + \frac{5}{6} + \frac{3}{8} + \frac{1}{6} =$

_____

Simplifying Fractions

(541) $\frac{72}{12}$ = _____

(542) $\frac{288}{54}$ = _____

(543) $\frac{330}{50}$ = _____

(544) $\frac{260}{56}$ = _____

(545) $\frac{1000}{120}$ = _____

(546) $\frac{126}{35}$ = _____

(547) $\frac{16}{24}$ = _____

(548) $\frac{123}{24}$ = _____

(549) $\frac{240}{30}$ = _____

(550) $\frac{80}{10}$ = _____

(551) $\frac{14}{21}$ = _____

(552) $\frac{315}{36}$ = _____

(553) $\frac{621}{108}$ = _____

(554) $\frac{129}{18}$ = _____

(555) $\frac{632}{80}$ = _____

(556) $\frac{630}{70}$ = _____

(557) $\frac{672}{96}$ = _____

(558) $\frac{96}{48}$ = _____

(559) $\frac{192}{24}$ = _____

(560) $\frac{12}{84}$ = _____

Simplifying Fractions

(561) $\frac{10}{20}$ = _____

(562) $\frac{225}{45}$ = _____

(563) $\frac{324}{36}$ = _____

(564) $\frac{200}{40}$ = _____

(565) $\frac{495}{126}$ = _____

(566) $\frac{60}{30}$ = _____

(567) $\frac{8}{12}$ = _____

(568) $\frac{432}{72}$ = _____

(569) $\frac{3}{15}$ = _____

(570) $\frac{200}{60}$ = _____

(571) $\frac{7}{28}$ = _____

(572) $\frac{27}{30}$ = _____

(573) $\frac{483}{98}$ = _____

(574) $\frac{153}{54}$ = _____

(575) $\frac{70}{20}$ = _____

(576) $\frac{100}{50}$ = _____

(577) $\frac{254}{30}$ = _____

(578) $\frac{30}{15}$ = _____

(579) $\frac{8}{64}$ = _____

(580) $\frac{30}{36}$ = _____

Name: _____

Date: ___/___/_____

Time Taken: _____ Min

Simplifying Fractions

581) $\dfrac{228}{24}$ = _____

582) $\dfrac{9}{45}$ = _____

583) $\dfrac{178}{30}$ = _____

584) $\dfrac{240}{40}$ = _____

585) $\dfrac{306}{72}$ = _____

586) $\dfrac{12}{20}$ = _____

587) $\dfrac{18}{27}$ = _____

588) $\dfrac{150}{75}$ = _____

589) $\dfrac{324}{48}$ = _____

590) $\dfrac{9}{12}$ = _____

591) $\dfrac{728}{98}$ = _____

592) $\dfrac{72}{36}$ = _____

593) $\dfrac{5}{25}$ = _____

594) $\dfrac{96}{48}$ = _____

595) $\dfrac{81}{12}$ = _____

596) $\dfrac{826}{98}$ = _____

597) $\dfrac{228}{72}$ = _____

598) $\dfrac{54}{18}$ = _____

599) $\dfrac{108}{48}$ = _____

600) $\dfrac{360}{60}$ = _____

Name: _____

Date: ___/___/___

Time Taken: ___ ___ Min

Simplifying Fractions

(601) $\frac{24}{6}$ = _____

(602) $\frac{525}{105}$ = _____

(603) $\frac{266}{28}$ = _____

(604) $\frac{150}{75}$ = _____

(605) $\frac{75}{9}$ = _____

(606) $\frac{300}{36}$ = _____

(607) $\frac{360}{90}$ = _____

(608) $\frac{4}{48}$ = _____

(609) $\frac{5}{70}$ = _____

(610) $\frac{45}{72}$ = _____

(611) $\frac{198}{30}$ = _____

(612) $\frac{36}{72}$ = _____

(613) $\frac{81}{135}$ = _____

(614) $\frac{35}{84}$ = _____

(615) $\frac{119}{21}$ = _____

(616) $\frac{18}{8}$ = _____

(617) $\frac{60}{70}$ = _____

(618) $\frac{78}{15}$ = _____

(619) $\frac{224}{24}$ = _____

(620) $\frac{117}{30}$ = _____

Simplifying Fractions

(621) $\frac{70}{10}$ = _____

(622) $\frac{40}{56}$ = _____

(623) $\frac{164}{24}$ = _____

(624) $\frac{70}{12}$ = _____

(625) $\frac{90}{18}$ = _____

(626) $\frac{104}{32}$ = _____

(627) $\frac{288}{72}$ = _____

(628) $\frac{81}{90}$ = _____

(629) $\frac{405}{45}$ = _____

(630) $\frac{28}{32}$ = _____

(631) $\frac{70}{21}$ = _____

(632) $\frac{36}{60}$ = _____

(633) $\frac{40}{120}$ = _____

(634) $\frac{693}{98}$ = _____

(635) $\frac{160}{20}$ = _____

(636) $\frac{126}{36}$ = _____

(637) $\frac{80}{20}$ = _____

(638) $\frac{252}{84}$ = _____

(639) $\frac{12}{24}$ = _____

(640) $\frac{56}{6}$ = _____

Name:

Date:
__/__/____

Time Taken:
____ Min

Associative Property

Use the associative property to fill the missing values.

641 (7 + 3) + _ = 1 + (_ + 3)

642 (7 × _) × 6 = (7 × _) × 2

643 7 + (6 + _) = (8 + _) + 6

644 7 + (3 + _) = (7 + 6) + _

645 2 + (6 + _) = (5 + _) + 6

646 3 + (_ + 7) = (6 + 3) + _

647 8 × (9 × _) = _ × (8 × 1)

648 (_ × 4) × 7 = (_ × 4) × 3

649 (3 + 2) + _ = (3 + 4) + _

650 5 + (9 + _) = 2 + (_ + 5)

651 4 + (3 + _) = _ + (9 + 4)

652 (6 × _) × 2 = 6 × (_ × 5)

Associative Property

Use the associative property to fill the missing values.

(653) 3 + (8 + __) = 4 + (__ + 8)

(654) __ × (5 × 7) = (3 × __) × 5

(655) 8 + (__ + 5) = (5 + __) + 4

(656) (4 × __) × 8 = 4 × (__ × 5)

(657) (5 + __) + 7 = 9 + (__ + 5)

(658) (__ × 3) × 7 = __ × (8 × 3)

(659) 4 + (__ + 7) = (4 + __) + 5

(660) 5 × (3 × __) = 4 × (5 × __)

(661) (7 + 4) + __ = (__ + 5) + 7

(662) 6 + (2 + __) = (1 + __) + 2

(663) (__ × 5) × 2 = (5 × __) × 6

(664) (8 + __) + 6 = __ + (6 + 7)

Associative Property

Use the associative property to fill the missing values.

(665) 7 + (8 + _) = _ + (7 + 6)

(666) (5 × _) × 6 = 5 × (_ × 3)

(667) (4 × 7) × _ = (7 × _) × 8

(668) _ × (6 × 7) = _ × (7 × 2)

(669) (4 + 8) + _ = (3 + 4) + _

(670) (3 + _) + 1 = _ + (8 + 3)

(671) 7 × (_ × 8) = (4 × _) × 8

(672) 7 + (4 + _) = (6 + 4) + _

(673) (4 + 7) + _ = 4 + (2 + _)

(674) (6 + 7) + _ = _ + (2 + 6)

(675) 6 × (7 × _) = (3 × _) × 7

(676) (_ × 9) × 8 = (_ × 8) × 2

Commutative Property

Use the commutative property to fill the missing values.

(677) 7 × 9 = 9 × __

(678) 9 + __ = 1 + 9

(679) 7 × 6 = __ × 7

(680) 8 + 5 = 5 + __

(681) 4 + __ = 6 + 4

(682) __ + 7 = 7 + 5

(683) 7 × 8 = __ × 7

(684) 1 × 4 = 4 × __

(685) __ × 5 = 5 × 7

(686) __ + 2 = 2 + 5

(687) 5 + __ = 6 + 5

(688) 3 + 2 = 2 + __

(689) 5 + 1 = __ + 5

(690) __ + 1 = 1 + 2

(691) 4 × 8 = 8 × __

(692) 8 × 4 = __ × 8

(693) 8 × 7 = __ × 8

(694) __ + 3 = 3 + 5

(695) __ + 8 = 8 + 1

(696) 4 + __ = 7 + 4

(697) 2 + 9 = 9 + __

(698) 6 + 9 = 9 + __

Commutative Property

Use the commutative property to fill the missing values.

(699) 2 + __ = 8 + 2

(700) 8 × __ = 5 × 8

(701) 3 + 8 = __ + 3

(702) 3 × 2 = __ × 3

(703) 4 × 2 = __ × 4

(704) 7 × 2 = __ × 7

(705) __ × 5 = 5 × 2

(706) __ + 2 = 2 + 6

(707) __ × 6 = 6 × 3

(708) 1 × 8 = __ × 1

(709) 4 + __ = 1 + 4

(710) 7 + 3 = 3 + __

(711) 7 + 5 = __ + 7

(712) __ × 6 = 6 × 8

(713) 2 × __ = 7 × 2

(714) 8 × 9 = __ × 8

(715) 6 + 7 = 7 + __

(716) __ + 4 = 4 + 5

(717) __ × 6 = 6 × 4

(718) 3 + 5 = __ + 3

(719) 9 + __ = 3 + 9

(720) __ × 8 = 8 × 4

Commutative Property

Use the commutative property to fill the missing values.

(721) 7 + 5 = __ + 7

(722) __ × 2 = 2 × 1

(723) 7 × __ = 3 × 7

(724) 7 × __ = 2 × 7

(725) 3 × __ = 9 × 3

(726) 2 × __ = 1 × 2

(727) __ × 7 = 7 × 4

(728) __ + 6 = 6 + 4

(729) 9 × 3 = 3 × __

(730) 5 × __ = 4 × 5

(731) 5 + __ = 3 + 5

(732) 4 + __ = 8 + 4

(733) __ + 8 = 8 + 2

(734) 2 + 4 = 4 + __

(735) 7 × __ = 8 × 7

(736) 2 + 3 = 3 + __

(737) __ + 2 = 2 + 6

(738) __ + 2 = 2 + 4

(739) __ × 3 = 3 × 4

(740) 9 + 8 = 8 + __

(741) 1 × 7 = __ × 1

(742) __ × 4 = 4 × 3

Name:
_____
Date:
__/__/____
Time Taken:
___ Min

Distributive Property

Use the distributive property to fill the missing values.

(743) (7 + __) × 2 = 2 × 7 + __ × 8

(744) __ × (5 + 1) = 2 × 5 + 2 × __

(745) (3 + __) × 4 = 4 × __ + 4 × 1

(746) (1 + 9) × __ = 6 × __ + 6 × 9

(747) 4 × (__ + 1) = 4 × 2 + 4 × __

(748) (2 + 8) × __ = 3 × 2 + 3 × __

(749) (__ + 3) × 7 = 7 × 6 + __ × 3

(750) (__ + 7) × 4 = 4 × 8 + __ × 7

(751) __ × (1 + 6) = 2 × __ + 2 × 6

(752) (__ + 2) × 1 = 1 × 7 + __ × 2

(753) 5 × (6 + __) = 5 × 6 + __ × 3

(754) 1 × (__ + 7) = 1 × 8 + 1 × __

Name:
....
Date:
__/__/____
Time Taken:
____ Min

Distributive Property

Use the distributive property to fill the missing values.

(755) (8 + 3) × __ = 4 × __ + 4 × 3

(756) 3 × (4 + __) = 3 × __ + 3 × 9

(757) 8 × (__ + 3) = 8 × 6 + 8 × __

(758) 2 × (1 + __) = 2 × 1 + __ × 4

(759) 3 × (4 + __) = 3 × 4 + __ × 2

(760) (2 + __) × 8 = 8 × 2 + __ × 6

(761) __ × (8 + 4) = 7 × 8 + 7 × __

(762) 6 × (1 + __) = 6 × 1 + __ × 8

(763) 8 × (__ + 7) = 8 × 5 + 8 × __

(764) (4 + __) × 8 = 8 × 4 + __ × 2

(765) (__ + 5) × 4 = 4 × 8 + __ × 5

(766) (9 + 7) × __ = 4 × 9 + 4 × __

Distributive Property

Use the distributive property to fill the missing values.

(767) (5 + __) × 2 = 2 × 5 + __ × 7

(768) 6 × (__ + 4) = 6 × 9 + 6 × __

(769) (2 + 4) × __ = 8 × __ + 8 × 4

(770) (3 + 7) × __ = 2 × 3 + 2 × __

(771) __ × (5 + 6) = 9 × __ + 9 × 6

(772) 3 × (__ + 2) = 3 × 5 + __ × 2

(773) (8 + 7) × __ = 4 × __ + 4 × 7

(774) 8 × (7 + __) = 8 × 7 + __ × 6

(775) (__ + 1) × 8 = 8 × 7 + 8 × __

(776) 7 × (__ + 5) = 7 × 4 + __ × 5

(777) (1 + 4) × __ = 5 × 1 + 5 × __

(778) (__ + 7) × 9 = 9 × 4 + 9 × __

Fast Math Success Workbook Grade 5-6

59

Name:
....

Date:
__/__/____

Time Taken:
_____ Min

Percent

Find the percentage of given numbers and percent values.

(779) 8% of ☐ = 32

(780) ☐ of 476 = 9.52

(781) 10% of ☐ = 34.9

(782) 5% of ☐ = 43.05

(783) 15% of ☐ = 4.95

(784) 20% of ☐ = 97.6

(785) 25% of ☐ = 70.5

(786) 8% of ☐ = 24.48

(787) 15% of 905 = ☐

(788) ☐ of 750 = 75

(789) ☐ of 689 = 13.78

(790) ☐ of 648 = 32.4

(791) 25% of ☐ = 51.75

(792) 20% of ☐ = 94

(793) 8% of ☐ = 36.88

(794) ☐ of 309 = 77.25

(795) ☐ of 327 = 32.7

(796) ☐ of 284 = 5.68

(797) 8% of ☐ = 23.76

(798) ☐ of 690 = 138

Name:

Date:
__/__/____

Time Taken:
____ Min

Percent

Find the percentage of given numbers and percent values.

(799) ☐ of 930 = 93   (800) 25% of ☐ = 118

(801) 15% of 141 = ☐   (802) 2% of ☐ = 16.54

(803) 8% of 285 = ☐   (804) 5% of 197 = ☐

(805) 10% of 690 = ☐   (806) 20% of 967 = ☐

(807) 25% of 648 = ☐   (808) ☐ of 481 = 120.25

(809) ☐ of 804 = 64.32   (810) 20% of 78 = ☐

(811) 15% of ☐ = 69.6   (812) 5% of ☐ = 29.1

(813) 10% of 129 = ☐   (814) 5% of ☐ = 21.6

(815) ☐ of 4 = 1   (816) 20% of 792 = ☐

(817) 10% of ☐ = 80.4   (818) 8% of 457 = ☐

Percent

Find the percentage of given numbers and percent values.

(819) ☐ of 123 = 24.6

(820) ☐ of 881 = 70.48

(821) 20% of 196 = ☐

(822) ☐ of 691 = 13.82

(823) 5% of 766 = ☐

(824) 25% of ☐ = 149.25

(825) ☐ of 375 = 30

(826) ☐ of 285 = 28.5

(827) 15% of 955 = ☐

(828) 2% of 850 = ☐

(829) 25% of 540 = ☐

(830) 5% of 649 = ☐

(831) 15% of 824 = ☐

(832) 8% of ☐ = 67.76

(833) ☐ of 642 = 128.4

(834) 10% of 321 = ☐

(835) ☐ of 26 = 6.5

(836) 10% of 171 = ☐

(837) 8% of 708 = ☐

(838) 15% of 173 = ☐

Percent

Find the percentage of given numbers and percent values.

(839) 5% of ☐ = 5.2

(840) 10% of 214 = ☐

(841) 2% of ☐ = 0.46

(842) 15% of 17 = ☐

(843) ☐ of 37 = 7.4

(844) ☐ of 77 = 6.16

(845) 10% of ☐ = 39.6

(846) 15% of 428 = ☐

(847) 20% of ☐ = 14.8

(848) ☐ of 872 = 17.44

(849) ☐ of 650 = 32.5

(850) 25% of ☐ = 53

(851) 8% of 179 = ☐

(852) 10% of 623 = ☐

(853) 25% of 712 = ☐

(854) ☐ of 295 = 5.9

(855) 5% of 86 = ☐

(856) 8% of ☐ = 72.64

(857) 15% of ☐ = 122.4

(858) 20% of ☐ = 158.6

Percent

Find the percentage of given numbers and percent values.

(859) 5% of ⬚ = 27.5

(860) 25% of 539 = ⬚

(861) 15% of 145 = ⬚

(862) 20% of 74 = ⬚

(863) ⬚ of 724 = 14.48

(864) ⬚ of 550 = 55

(865) ⬚ of 345 = 27.6

(866) 10% of 655 = ⬚

(867) 8% of ⬚ = 34.64

(868) 5% of 552 = ⬚

(869) ⬚ of 241 = 4.82

(870) ⬚ of 747 = 149.4

(871) ⬚ of 197 = 29.55

(872) 25% of ⬚ = 181.25

(873) ⬚ of 316 = 31.6

(874) 5% of ⬚ = 10.3

(875) 25% of ⬚ = 54

(876) 20% of 108 = ⬚

(877) 8% of 728 = ⬚

(878) 2% of ⬚ = 2.38

Name:

Date:
__/__/____

Time Taken:
_____ Min

Percent and Decimals

Convert Percent to Decimal.

(879) 7 % =
_____

(880) 71 % =
_____

(881) 72 % =
_____

(882) 69 % =
_____

(883) 3 % =
_____

(884) 73 % =
_____

(885) 37 % =
_____

(886) 32 % =
_____

(887) 44 % =
_____

(888) 41 % =
_____

(889) 24 % =
_____

(890) 49 % =
_____

(891) 79 % =
_____

(892) 58 % =
_____

(893) 14 % =
_____

(894) 6 % =
_____

(895) 91 % =
_____

(896) 67 % =
_____

(897) 83 % =
_____

(898) 16 % =
_____

Percent and Decimals

Convert Percent to Decimal.

(899) 3 % = _____

(900) 22 % = _____

(901) 66 % = _____

(902) 78 % = _____

(903) 65 % = _____

(904) 1 % = _____

(905) 13 % = _____

(906) 67 % = _____

(907) 74 % = _____

(908) 25 % = _____

(909) 87 % = _____

(910) 85 % = _____

(911) 6 % = _____

(912) 7 % = _____

(913) 81 % = _____

(914) 61 % = _____

(915) 77 % = _____

(916) 19 % = _____

(917) 18 % = _____

(918) 52 % = _____

Name:

Date:
__/__/____
Time Taken:
_____ Min

Percent and Decimals

Convert Decimal to Percent.

(919) 0.79 = _____

(920) 0.42 = _____

(921) 0.02 = _____

(922) 0.86 = _____

(923) 0.98 = _____

(924) 0.5 = _____

(925) 0.4 = _____

(926) 0.99 = _____

(927) 0.54 = _____

(928) 0.17 = _____

(929) 0.52 = _____

(930) 0.75 = _____

(931) 0.24 = _____

(932) 0.19 = _____

(933) 0.31 = _____

(934) 0.3 = _____

(935) 0.95 = _____

(936) 0.73 = _____

(937) 0.49 = _____

(938) 0.43 = _____

Percent and Decimals
Convert Decimal to Percent.

(939) 0.19 = _____

(940) 0.75 = _____

(941) 0.13 = _____

(942) 0.58 = _____

(943) 0.17 = _____

(944) 0.23 = _____

(945) 0.14 = _____

(946) 0.3 = _____

(947) 0.74 = _____

(948) 0.61 = _____

(949) 0.22 = _____

(950) 0.91 = _____

(951) 0.79 = _____

(952) 0.88 = _____

(953) 0.07 = _____

(954) 0.76 = _____

(955) 0.69 = _____

(956) 0.28 = _____

(957) 0.92 = _____

(958) 0.98 = _____

Percent and Decimals

Convert Decimal to Percent.

(959) 0.98 = _____

(960) 0.14 = _____

(961) 0.07 = _____

(962) 0.21 = _____

(963) 0.13 = _____

(964) 0.38 = _____

(965) 0.8 = _____

(966) 0.68 = _____

(967) 0.48 = _____

(968) 0.9 = _____

(969) 0.36 = _____

(970) 0.23 = _____

(971) 0.28 = _____

(972) 0.74 = _____

(973) 0.4 = _____

(974) 0.33 = _____

(975) 0.17 = _____

(976) 0.86 = _____

(977) 0.24 = _____

(978) 0.43 = _____

Percent and Decimals

Convert Decimal to Percent.

(979) 0.91 = _____

(980) 0.53 = _____

(981) 0.34 = _____

(982) 0.41 = _____

(983) 0.43 = _____

(984) 0.07 = _____

(985) 0.81 = _____

(986) 0.05 = _____

(987) 0.21 = _____

(988) 0.52 = _____

(989) 0.22 = _____

(990) 0.78 = _____

(991) 0.99 = _____

(992) 0.51 = _____

(993) 0.96 = _____

(994) 0.11 = _____

(995) 0.76 = _____

(996) 0.06 = _____

(997) 0.48 = _____

(998) 0.74 = _____

Percent - Advanced

Calculate the given percent of each value.

(999) 0.1% of [ ] = 0.071

(1000) 4.2% of [ ] = 30.66

(1001) [ ] of 6 = 0.588

(1002) 0.2% of [ ] = 0.102

(1003) 6.8% of [ ] = 0.408

(1004) [ ] of 478 = 34.416

(1005) 0.9% of 467 = [ ]

(1006) 4.4% of [ ] = 41.36

(1007) 0.7% of 68 = [ ]

(1008) [ ] of 34 = 0.068

(1009) 3.8% of 118 = [ ]

(1010) 0.1% of 435 = [ ]

(1011) [ ] of 7 = 0.35

(1012) [ ] of 89 = 8.188

(1013) 1.7% of 85 = [ ]

(1014) [ ] of 38 = 0.95

(1015) 0.7% of [ ] = 0.056

(1016) 0.6% of [ ] = 0.018

(1017) 0.7% of [ ] = 0.392

(1018) [ ] of 56 = 4.76

Percent - Advanced

Calculate the given percent of each value.

(1019) 0.7% of 5 = ☐

(1020) 0.1% of 4 = ☐

(1021) 0.4% of 4 = ☐

(1022) 0.8% of 113 = ☐

(1023) ☐ of 6 = 0.048

(1024) 5.2% of 4 = ☐

(1025) 0.7% of ☐ = 0.469

(1026) ☐ of 2 = 0.022

(1027) 0.1% of ☐ = 0.006

(1028) 1.1% of 5 = ☐

(1029) ☐ of 971 = 74.767

(1030) 5.1% of 2 = ☐

(1031) 0.2% of ☐ = 0.006

(1032) ☐ of 852 = 2.556

(1033) ☐ of 69 = 6.279

(1034) 2.6% of ☐ = 16.172

(1035) 0.7% of ☐ = 0.266

(1036) ☐ of 85 = 7.48

(1037) 1.9% of 751 = ☐

(1038) ☐ of 421 = 3.789

Percent - Advanced

Calculate the given percent of each value.

(1039) 2.5% of ☐ = 19.375

(1040) 0.9% of ☐ = 2.241

(1041) 4.8% of ☐ = 4.128

(1042) 7.6% of ☐ = 0.684

(1043) 2.9% of 7 = ☐

(1044) 0.3% of 2 = ☐

(1045) 9.9% of ☐ = 5.049

(1046) 9.0% of 997 = ☐

(1047) 6.1% of 41 = ☐

(1048) ☐ of 842 = 30.312

(1049) ☐ of 17 = 0.102

(1050) 0.6% of 64 = ☐

(1051) ☐ of 56 = 0.056

(1052) 9.4% of ☐ = 38.916

(1053) 0.9% of ☐ = 0.783

(1054) ☐ of 2 = 0.004

(1055) ☐ of 548 = 1.644

(1056) 6.3% of ☐ = 0.378

(1057) 7.9% of ☐ = 7.189

(1058) 5.7% of ☐ = 1.71

Name:
_____
Date:
___/___/____
Time Taken:
_____ Min

Percent - Advanced

Calculate the given percent of each value.

(1059) 6.8% of [   ] = 0.204

(1060) [   ] of 375 = 1.125

(1061) [   ] of 529 = 8.993

(1062) [   ] of 525 = 1.05

(1063) 2.8% of [   ] = 2.156

(1064) 2.9% of 437 = [   ]

(1065) 7.3% of [   ] = 2.774

(1066) 0.9% of [   ] = 0.378

(1067) 4.4% of [   ] = 36.784

(1068) 3.9% of [   ] = 1.872

(1069) 5.9% of 483 = [   ]

(1070) 3.3% of 5 = [   ]

(1071) 8.7% of 8 = [   ]

(1072) 9.4% of [   ] = 0.658

(1073) [   ] of 95 = 1.33

(1074) 0.9% of [   ] = 0.639

(1075) 3.0% of [   ] = 0.93

(1076) 7.9% of [   ] = 0.158

(1077) 0.4% of [   ] = 2.716

(1078) 0.2% of [   ] = 0.15

Percent - Advanced

Calculate the given percent of each value.

(1079) 4.6% of 440 = [   ]

(1080) [   ] of 33 = 1.881

(1081) 0.8% of [   ] = 0.536

(1082) 9.6% of [   ] = 71.52

(1083) [   ] of 2 = 0.008

(1084) [   ] of 632 = 46.768

(1085) 4.9% of [   ] = 47.628

(1086) 6.2% of 388 = [   ]

(1087) 0.7% of [   ] = 0.014

(1088) [   ] of 483 = 15.939

(1089) 0.9% of [   ] = 0.027

(1090) 1.6% of 307 = [   ]

(1091) 1.2% of [   ] = 0.024

(1092) 7.9% of [   ] = 3.95

(1093) 6.3% of 950 = [   ]

(1094) 3.8% of 9 = [   ]

(1095) 3.6% of 278 = [   ]

(1096) 8.8% of [   ] = 7.92

(1097) 0.6% of 2 = [   ]

(1098) 1.2% of 1 = [   ]

Ratio Conversions

Provide the conversions for each ratio (Part to Part).

(1099)

	Ratio	Fraction	Percent	Decimal
a.	3:3			
b.	2:7			
c.	1:10			
d.	2:5			
e.	2:4			
f.	2:10			
g.	5:7			
h.	1:8			
i.	3:5			
j.	1:2			
k.	4:7			
l.	2:9			
m.	5:6			

Ratio Conversions

Provide the conversions for each ratio (Part to Part).

1100		Ratio	Fraction	Percent	Decimal
	a.	4:5			
	b.	2:2			
	c.	4:9			
	d.	2:10			
	e.	3:5			
	f.	6:8			
	g.	1:3			
	h.	2:6			
	i.	4:7			
	j.	5:8			
	k.	3:9			
	l.	5:10			
	m.	4:10			

Ratio Conversions

Provide the conversions for each ratio (Part to Part).

1101		Ratio	Fraction	Percent	Decimal
	a.	5:8			
	b.	5:9			
	c.	1:1			
	d.	5:10			
	e.	2:7			
	f.	7:8			
	g.	5:6			
	h.	1:8			
	i.	8:9			
	j.	4:9			
	k.	6:7			
	l.	1:2			
	m.	2:9			

Ratio Conversions

Provide the conversions for each ratio (Part to Part).

1102		Ratio	Fraction	Percent	Decimal
	a.	8:9			
	b.				1
	c.		3/8		
	d.	2:7			
	e.	1:10			
	f.		1/6		
	g.				0.7
	h.		1/5		
	i.				0.5
	j.		4/6		
	k.		4/7		
	l.				0.333
	m.			80%	

Name:
_____

Date:
__/__/____

Time Taken:
_____ Min

Cartesian Coordinates

Fill in as indicated.

(1103)

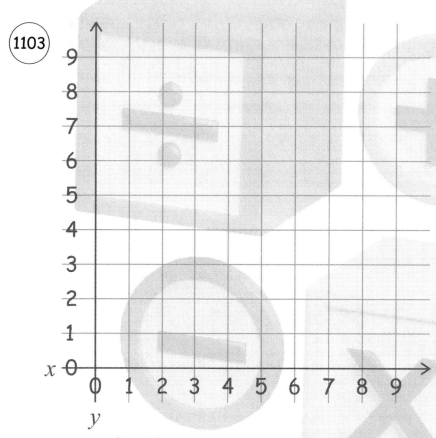

A = (7, 7)   B = (9, 9)

C = (1, 6)   D = (7, 5)

E = (5, 2)   F = (2, 8)

G = (2, 1)   H = (4, 1)

I = (7, 1)   J = (6, 0)

Cartesian Coordinates

Fill in as indicated.

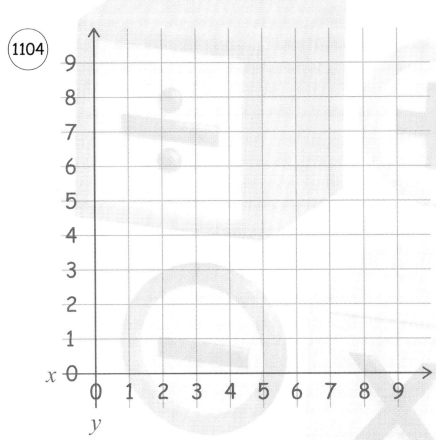

(1104)

A = (6, 6)   B = (5, 6)

C = (0, 1)   D = (2, 1)

E = (7, 6)   F = (2, 7)

G = (1, 4)   H = (1, 9)

I = (7, 1)   J = (9, 3)

Cartesian Coordinates

Fill in as indicated.

(1105)

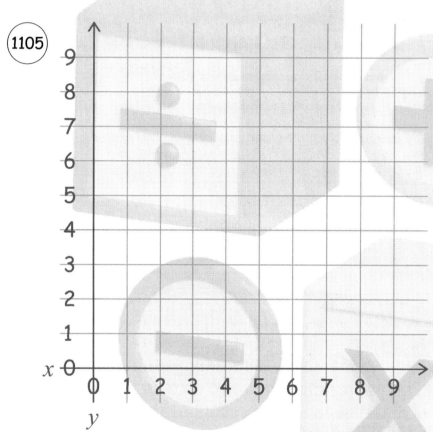

A = (6, 6)   B = (5, 3)

C = (2, 8)   D = (8, 4)

E = (0, 2)   F = (0, 5)

G = (1, 9)   H = (2, 4)

I = (0, 1)   J = (4, 4)

Name:

Date:
__/__/____

Time Taken:
___ Min

Cartesian Coordinates

Fill in as indicated.

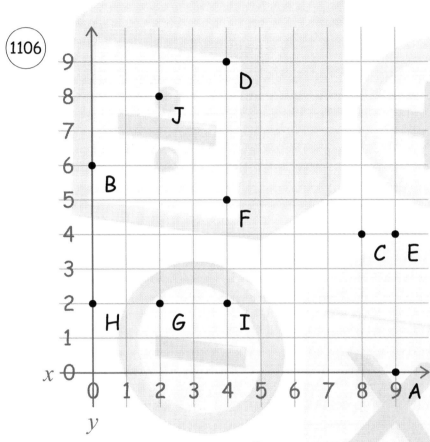

(1106)

A = _____   B = _____

C = _____   D = _____

E = _____   F = _____

G = _____   H = _____

I = _____   J = _____

Cartesian Coordinates

Fill in as indicated.

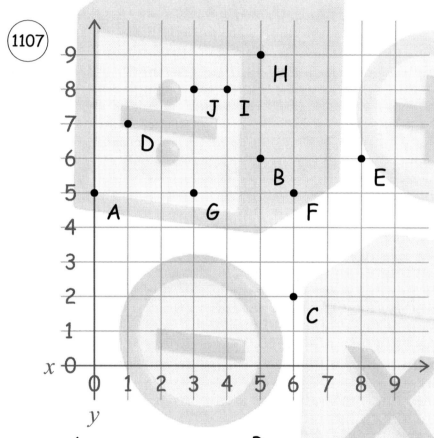

(1107)

A = _____   B = _____

C = _____   D = _____

E = _____   F = _____

G = _____   H = _____

I = _____   J = _____

Name:

Date:
___/___/___

Time Taken:
____ Min

Cartesian Coordinates

Fill in as indicated.

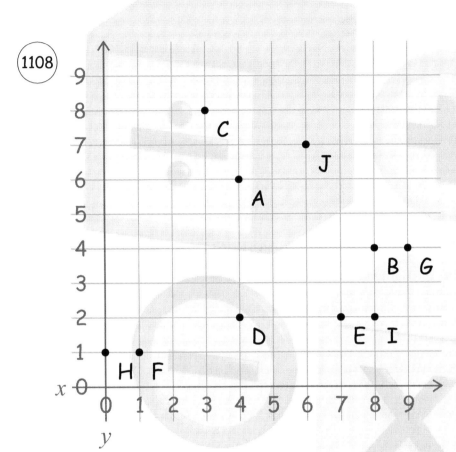

A = _____   B = _____

C = _____   D = _____

E = _____   F = _____

G = _____   H = _____

I = _____   J = _____

Cartesian Coordinates With Four Quadrants

Fill in as indicated.

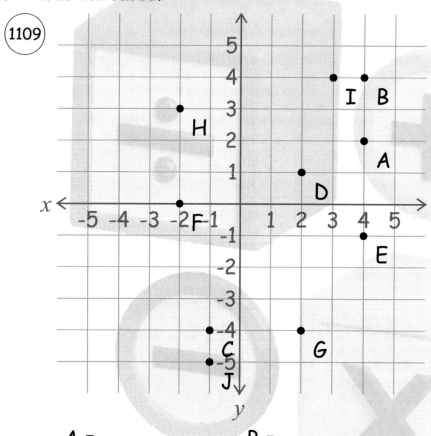

(1109)

A = _____   B = _____

C = _____   D = _____

E = _____   F = _____

G = _____   H = _____

I = _____   J = _____

Name:

Date:
__/__/____

Time Taken:
____ Min

Cartesian Coordinates With Four Quadrants

Fill in as indicated.

(1110)

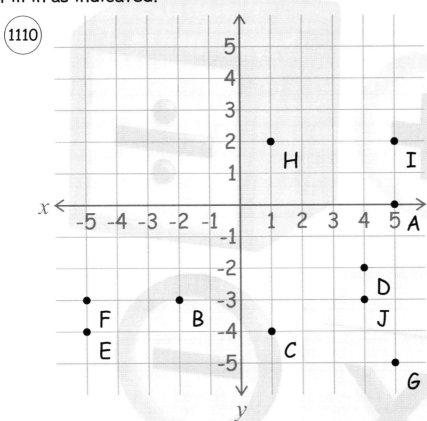

A = _____ B = _____

C = _____ D = _____

E = _____ F = _____

G = _____ H = _____

I = _____ J = _____

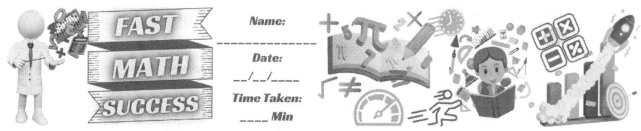

Cartesian Coordinates With Four Quadrants

Fill in as indicated.

(1111)

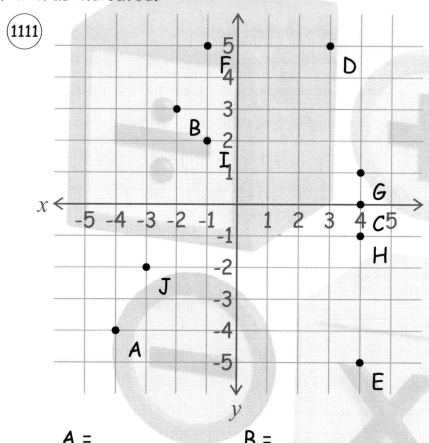

A = _____   B = _____

C = _____   D = _____

E = _____   F = _____

G = _____   H = _____

I = _____   J = _____

Name:
_____

Date:
__/__/____

Time Taken:
___ . ___ Min

Cartesian Coordinates With Four Quadrants

Fill in as indicated.

(1112)

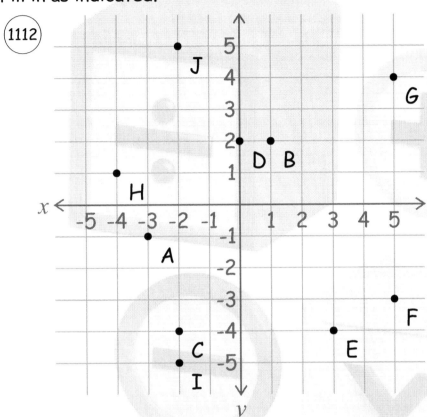

A = _____   B = _____

C = _____   D = _____

E = _____   F = _____

G = _____   H = _____

I = _____   J = _____

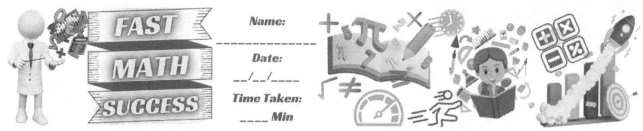

Name: _____
Date: ___/___/_____
Time Taken: _____ Min

Cartesian Coordinates With Four Quadrants

Fill in as indicated.

(1113)

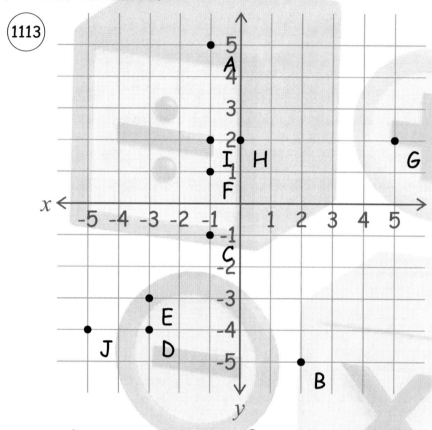

A = _____   B = _____

C = _____   D = _____

E = _____   F = _____

G = _____   H = _____

I = _____   J = _____

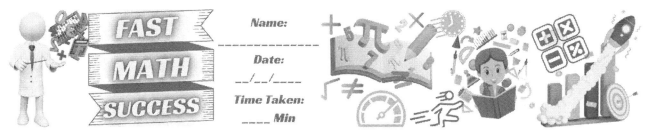

Cartesian Coordinates With Four Quadrants

Fill in as indicated.

(1114)

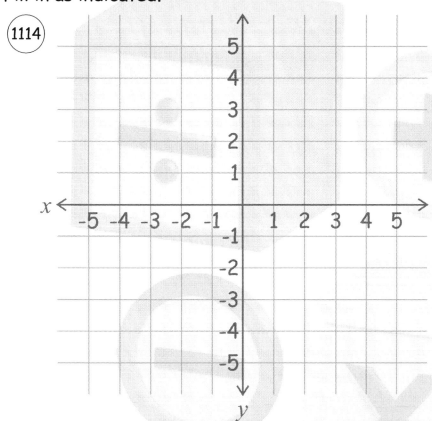

A = (-2, -3)   B = (-3, -2)

C = (5, 2)   D = (1, -5)

E = (-2, 4)   F = (-2, -4)

G = (5, -2)   H = (-5, 2)

I = (3, -5)   J = (-1, 0)

Cartesian Coordinates With Four Quadrants

Fill in as indicated.

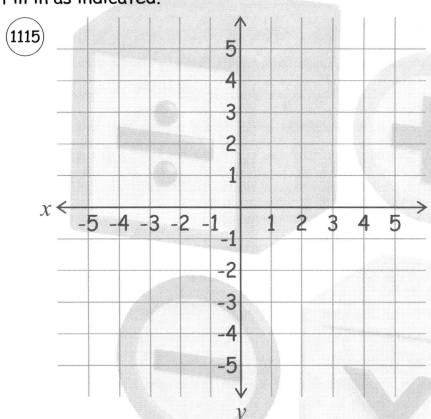

(1115)

A = (-1, 0)   B = (3, -1)

C = (-3, -3)   D = (-2, 0)

E = (-4, 2)   F = (-5, -3)

G = (1, -3)   H = (2, -1)

I = (-5, 3)   J = (3, -3)

Cartesian Coordinates With Four Quadrants

Fill in as indicated.

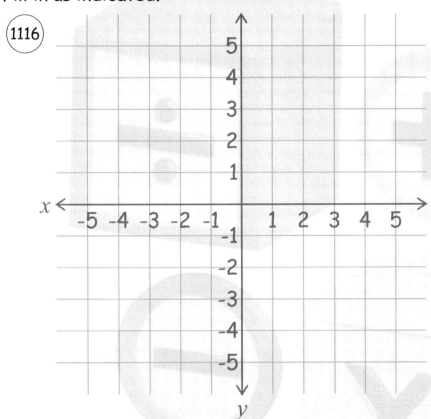

(1116)

A = (3, -1)   B = (5, -3)

C = (1, 2)   D = (2, 4)

E = (2, -4)   F = (5, -5)

G = (3, 2)   H = (0, 1)

I = (-1, -1)   J = (2, 2)

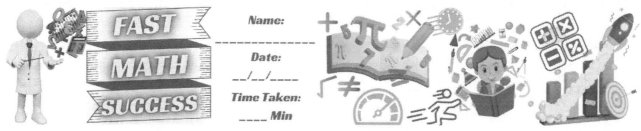
Cartesian Coordinates With Four Quadrants

Fill in as indicated.

(1117)

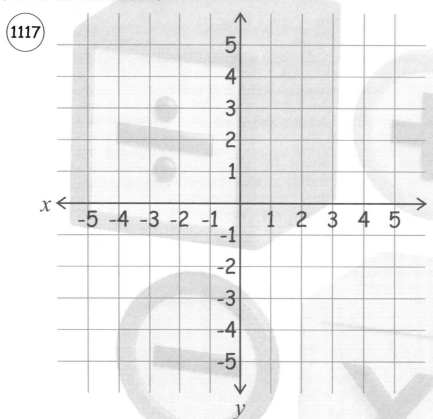

A = (-4, 3)   B = (2, 3)

C = (5, 1)   D = (-3, 5)

E = (-3, -3)   F = (2, -5)

G = (1, 0)   H = (3, 1)

I = (4, -5)   J = (2, 5)

Cartesian Coordinates With Four Quadrants

Fill in as indicated.

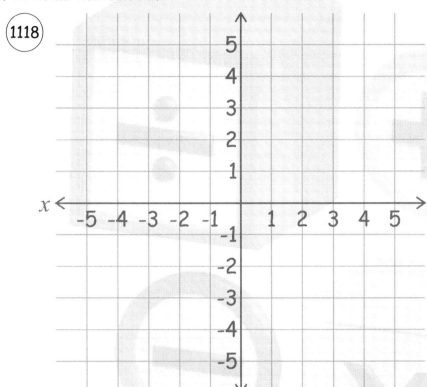

1118

$A = (0, 3)$ $B = (0, 5)$

$C = (4, 0)$ $D = (-2, -1)$

$E = (2, -3)$ $F = (-5, 4)$

$G = (5, 4)$ $H = (4, -5)$

$I = (5, 5)$ $J = (3, 0)$

Plot Lines

Plot and draw the lines.

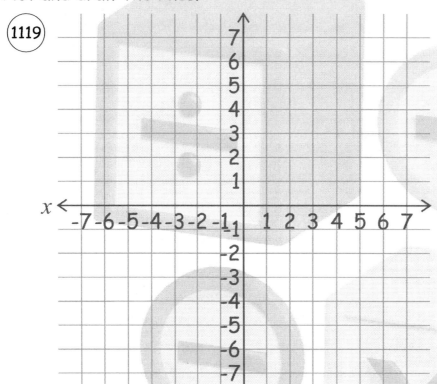

(1119)

A = (5, -7)   B = (-2, 7)

C = (2, -1)   D = (3, -3)

E = (0, 3)   F = (1, 1)

Plot Lines

Plot and draw the lines.

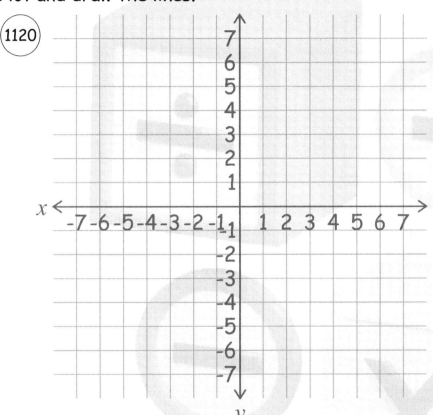

(1120)

A = (6, 1)   B = (0, 7)

C = (7, 0)   D = (5, 2)

E = (4, 3)   F = (3, 4)

Plot Lines

Plot and draw the lines.

(1121)

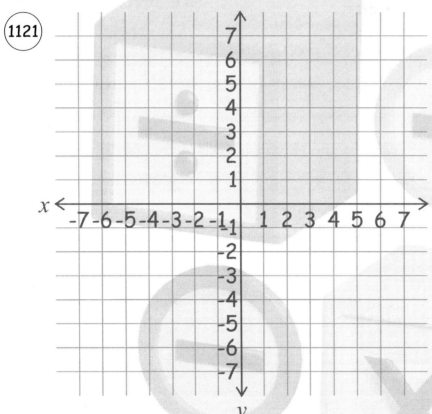

A = (-5, -1)   B = (-2, 2)

C = (-7, -3)   D = (3, 7)

E = (-6, -2)   F = (-4, 0)

Plot Lines

Plot and draw the lines.

(1122)

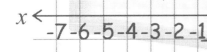
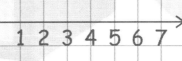

A = (3, 6)   B = (-5, -2)

C = (4, 7)   D = (-3, 0)

E = (-4, -1)   F = (0, 3)

Plot Lines

Plot and draw the lines.

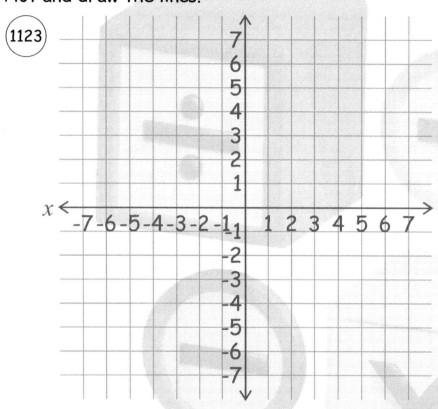

(1123)

A = (-3, 1)   B = (-5, 3)

C = (2, -4)   D = (-7, 5)

E = (0, -2)   F = (5, -7)

Plot Lines

Plot and draw the lines.

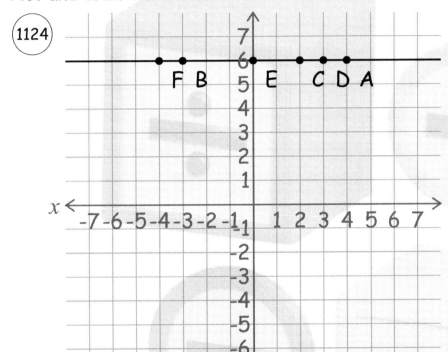

A = _____   B = _____

C = _____   D = _____

E = _____   F = _____

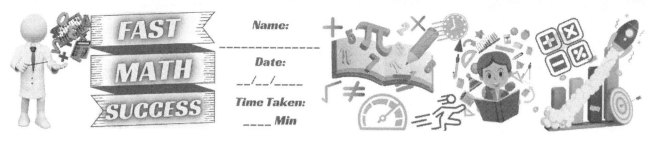

Plot Lines

Plot and draw the lines.

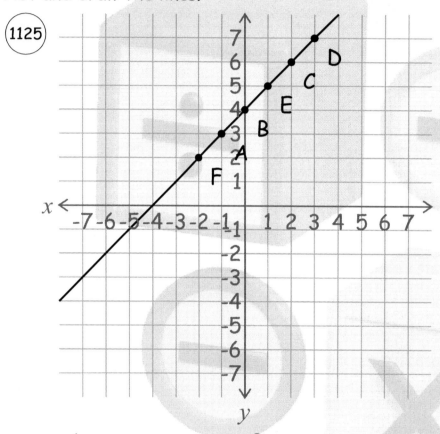

(1125)

A = _____   B = _____

C = _____   D = _____

E = _____   F = _____

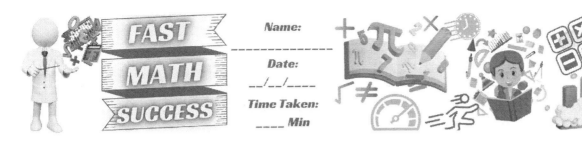
Plot Lines

Plot and draw the lines.

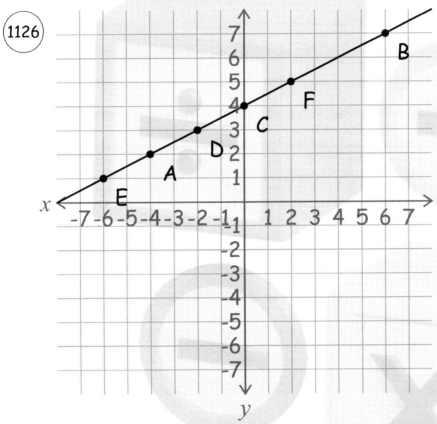

A = _____   B = _____

C = _____   D = _____

E = _____   F = _____

Name:

Date:
__/__/____

Time Taken:
____ Min

Plot Lines

Plot and draw the lines.

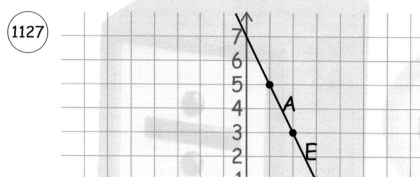

(1127)

A = _____   B = _____

C = _____   D = _____

E = _____   F = _____

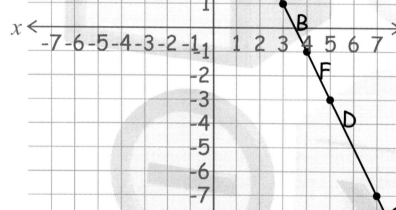

Name:
_____
Date:
__/__/____
Time Taken:
_____ Min

Plot Lines

Plot and draw the lines.

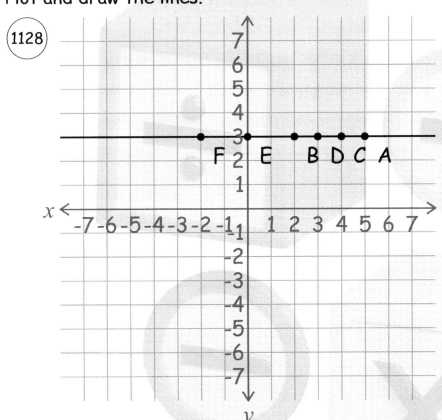

(1128)

A = _____   B = _____

C = _____   D = _____

E = _____   F = _____

Exponents

Convert the values.

(1129) $30^3 =$ _____

(1130) $85^2 =$ _____

(1131) $6^3 =$ _____

(1132) $38^3 =$ _____

(1133) $24^2 =$ _____

(1134) $59^3 =$ _____

(1135) $84^3 =$ _____

(1136) $79^3 =$ _____

(1137) $39^3 =$ _____

(1138) $34^2 =$ _____

(1139) $82^3 =$ _____

(1140) $88^3 =$ _____

(1141) $33^3 =$ _____

(1142) $91^2 =$ _____

(1143) $24^3 =$ _____

(1144) $18^2 =$ _____

(1145) $7^3 =$ _____

(1146) $72^3 =$ _____

(1147) $98^2 =$ _____

(1148) $87^2 =$ _____

Exponents

Convert the values.

(1149) $38^3 = $ _____

(1150) $9^2 = $ _____

(1151) $62^2 = $ _____

(1152) $16^3 = $ _____

(1153) $12^2 = $ _____

(1154) $76^2 = $ _____

(1155) $39^2 = $ _____

(1156) $92^2 = $ _____

(1157) $52^2 = $ _____

(1158) $2^3 = $ _____

(1159) $32^3 = $ _____

(1160) $53^2 = $ _____

(1161) $50^2 = $ _____

(1162) $38^2 = $ _____

(1163) $61^2 = $ _____

(1164) $21^2 = $ _____

(1165) $73^3 = $ _____

(1166) $3^3 = $ _____

(1167) $84^3 = $ _____

(1168) $74^3 = $ _____

Exponents

Convert the values.

(1169) $11^3 =$ _____

(1170) $28^2 =$ _____

(1171) $52^3 =$ _____

(1172) $58^3 =$ _____

(1173) $86^2 =$ _____

(1174) $74^3 =$ _____

(1175) $83^3 =$ _____

(1176) $34^3 =$ _____

(1177) $20^2 =$ _____

(1178) $63^2 =$ _____

(1179) $15^2 =$ _____

(1180) $65^2 =$ _____

(1181) $92^2 =$ _____

(1182) $64^2 =$ _____

(1183) $70^3 =$ _____

(1184) $71^2 =$ _____

(1185) $44^2 =$ _____

(1186) $91^2 =$ _____

(1187) $18^3 =$ _____

(1188) $96^3 =$ _____

Exponents

Convert the values.

(1189) 29^3 = _____

(1190) 61^3 = _____

(1191) 30^3 = _____

(1192) 26^2 = _____

(1193) 26^3 = _____

(1194) 51^2 = _____

(1195) 59^2 = _____

(1196) 95^3 = _____

(1197) 1^3 = _____

(1198) 65^2 = _____

(1199) 52^3 = _____

(1200) 67^3 = _____

(1201) 54^2 = _____

(1202) 81^2 = _____

(1203) 31^2 = _____

(1204) 23^3 = _____

(1205) 41^3 = _____

(1206) 34^2 = _____

(1207) 89^2 = _____

(1208) 84^2 = _____

Exponents

Convert the values.

(1209) $54^3 =$ _____

(1210) $6^3 =$ _____

(1211) $55^3 =$ _____

(1212) $99^3 =$ _____

(1213) $73^2 =$ _____

(1214) $75^2 =$ _____

(1215) $6^2 =$ _____

(1216) $13^3 =$ _____

(1217) $67^2 =$ _____

(1218) $45^3 =$ _____

(1219) $98^3 =$ _____

(1220) $61^2 =$ _____

(1221) $87^3 =$ _____

(1222) $10^3 =$ _____

(1223) $5^3 =$ _____

(1224) $44^2 =$ _____

(1225) $4^3 =$ _____

(1226) $35^3 =$ _____

(1227) $63^2 =$ _____

(1228) $33^2 =$ _____

Scientific Notation

Provide the scientific notation for each value.

(1229) 7,608,000 = _____

(1230) 5,733,000 = _____

(1231) 9,900,000 = _____

(1232) 6,600,000 = _____

(1233) 8,500,000 = _____

(1234) 9,141,000 = _____

(1235) 260,000 = _____

(1236) 5,740,000 = _____

(1237) 5,712,000 = _____

(1238) 7,310,000 = _____

(1239) 9,070,000 = _____

(1240) 3,674,000 = _____

(1241) 4,533,000 = _____

(1242) 5,826,000 = _____

(1243) 8,420,000 = _____

(1244) 6,429,000 = _____

(1245) 1,200,000 = _____

(1246) 2,988,000 = _____

(1247) 4,197,000 = _____

(1248) 7,600,000 = _____

Scientific Notation

Provide the scientific notation for each value.

(1249) 4,630,000 = _____

(1250) 6,006,000 = _____

(1251) 6,900,000 = _____

(1252) 694,000 = _____

(1253) 8,680,000 = _____

(1254) 7,700,000 = _____

(1255) 9,000,000 = _____

(1256) 4,200,000 = _____

(1257) 3,020,000 = _____

(1258) 4,600,000 = _____

(1259) 5,007,000 = _____

(1260) 1,800,000 = _____

(1261) 6,011,000 = _____

(1262) 6,595,000 = _____

(1263) 9,081,000 = _____

(1264) 796,000 = _____

(1265) 9,632,000 = _____

(1266) 1,900,000 = _____

(1267) 8,730,000 = _____

(1268) 2,120,000 = _____

Name:
_____

Date:
___/___/____

Time Taken:
_____ Min

Scientific Notation

Provide the scientific notation for each value.

(1269) 7,778,000 = _____   (1270) 1,200,000 = _____

(1271) 8,830,000 = _____   (1272) 586,000 = _____

(1273) 7,800,000 = _____   (1274) 5,745,000 = _____

(1275) 3,430,000 = _____   (1276) 4,746,000 = _____

(1277) 4,520,000 = _____   (1278) 1,357,000 = _____

(1279) 4,300,000 = _____   (1280) 9,200,000 = _____

(1281) 4,500,000 = _____   (1282) 500,000 = _____

(1283) 1,300,000 = _____   (1284) 4,137,000 = _____

(1285) 3,651,000 = _____   (1286) 5,424,000 = _____

(1287) 3,053,000 = _____   (1288) 8,938,000 = _____

Name:

Date:
__/__/____

Time Taken:
____ Min

Scientific Notation

Provide the scientific notation for each value.

(1289) $2.51 \times 10^5 =$ _____

(1290) $1.2 \times 10^6 =$ _____

(1291) $4.19 \times 10^6 =$ _____

(1292) $2.81 \times 10^6 =$ _____

(1293) $8.13 \times 10^6 =$ _____

(1294) $4.94 \times 10^6 =$ _____

(1295) $9.28 \times 10^6 =$ _____

(1296) $8.206 \times 10^6 =$ _____

(1297) $8.478 \times 10^6 =$ _____

(1298) $5.796 \times 10^6 =$ _____

(1299) $6.67 \times 10^6 =$ _____

(1300) $5.981 \times 10^6 =$ _____

(1301) $3 \times 10^6 =$ _____

(1302) $2.518 \times 10^6 =$ _____

(1303) $2.51 \times 10^6 =$ _____

(1304) $1 \times 10^6 =$ _____

(1305) $8.48 \times 10^6 =$ _____

(1306) $2.2 \times 10^6 =$ _____

(1307) $4.7 \times 10^5 =$ _____

(1308) $5.976 \times 10^6 =$ _____

FAST MATH SUCCESS

Name:
_____
Date:
__ / __ / ____
Time Taken:
____ Min

Scientific Notation

Provide the scientific notation for each value.

(1309) $8.657 \times 10^6 =$ _____

(1310) $3.428 \times 10^6 =$ _____

(1311) $1.77 \times 10^6 =$ _____

(1312) $1.758 \times 10^6 =$ _____

(1313) $9.32 \times 10^6 =$ _____

(1314) $3.5 \times 10^5 =$ _____

(1315) $3.918 \times 10^6 =$ _____

(1316) $1.93 \times 10^6 =$ _____

(1317) $2.9 \times 10^6 =$ _____

(1318) $2.3 \times 10^5 =$ _____

(1319) $9.43 \times 10^5 =$ _____

(1320) $1.4 \times 10^6 =$ _____

(1321) $3.5 \times 10^6 =$ _____

(1322) $6.21 \times 10^6 =$ _____

(1323) $2.936 \times 10^6 =$ _____

(1324) $9.087 \times 10^6 =$ _____

(1325) $2.688 \times 10^6 =$ _____

(1326) $4.59 \times 10^5 =$ _____

(1327) $7.2 \times 10^6 =$ _____

(1328) $6.3 \times 10^5 =$ _____

Scientific Notation

Provide the scientific notation for each value.

(1329) $7.88 \times 10^6 =$ _____

(1330) $5.331 \times 10^6 =$ _____

(1331) $7.723 \times 10^6 =$ _____

(1332) $3.776 \times 10^6 =$ _____

(1333) $7.324 \times 10^6 =$ _____

(1334) $1.08 \times 10^6 =$ _____

(1335) $6 \times 10^6 =$ _____

(1336) $5.8 \times 10^6 =$ _____

(1337) $5.983 \times 10^6 =$ _____

(1338) $3.608 \times 10^6 =$ _____

(1339) $5.4 \times 10^6 =$ _____

(1340) $6.7 \times 10^6 =$ _____

(1341) $1.69 \times 10^6 =$ _____

(1342) $9.3 \times 10^6 =$ _____

(1343) $1.01 \times 10^6 =$ _____

(1344) $4.949 \times 10^6 =$ _____

(1345) $1.171 \times 10^6 =$ _____

(1346) $7.7 \times 10^6 =$ _____

(1347) $7.115 \times 10^6 =$ _____

(1348) $5.582 \times 10^6 =$ _____

Name:

Date:
__/__/____

Time Taken:
____ Min

Expressions - Single Step

Solve for the variable.

(1349) $5 + x = 14$ _____

(1350) $x - 8 = -3$ _____

(1351) $7 - x = 6$ _____

(1352) $7 + x = 15$ _____

(1353) $2 - x = 0$ _____

(1354) $x - 6 = 1$ _____

(1355) $x + 4 = 12$ _____

(1356) $x + 5 = 12$ _____

(1357) $x - 9 = -4$ _____

(1358) $x + 5 = 10$ _____

(1359) $x + 9 = 15$ _____

(1360) $7 + x = 16$ _____

(1361) $x + 6 = 12$ _____

(1362) $x - 8 = -6$ _____

(1363) $x + 8 = 10$ _____

(1364) $4 - x = -4$ _____

(1365) $x - 1 = 3$ _____

(1366) $x + 6 = 10$ _____

(1367) $x + 1 = 9$ _____

(1368) $x - 8 = 1$ _____

Fast Math Success Workbook Grade 5-6

Expressions - Single Step

Solve for the variable.

(1369) $8 - x = 5$ _____

(1370) $1 - x = -5$ _____

(1371) $4 + x = 5$ _____

(1372) $x - 7 = -4$ _____

(1373) $4 - x = -4$ _____

(1374) $4 - x = 2$ _____

(1375) $x + 8 = 16$ _____

(1376) $9 - x = 2$ _____

(1377) $x + 6 = 10$ _____

(1378) $x + 4 = 10$ _____

(1379) $3 + x = 12$ _____

(1380) $x - 6 = 2$ _____

(1381) $9 - x = 8$ _____

(1382) $7 + x = 8$ _____

(1383) $3 - x = -5$ _____

(1384) $1 + x = 2$ _____

(1385) $x + 6 = 9$ _____

(1386) $x - 2 = 6$ _____

(1387) $9 + x = 16$ _____

(1388) $x + 5 = 12$ _____

Name: _____

Date: __/__/____

Time Taken: _____ Min

Expressions - Single Step

Solve for the variable.

(1389)	$2 - x = -3$ _____	(1390)	$x - 7 = 2$ _____
(1391)	$1 + x = 9$ _____	(1392)	$2 + x = 7$ _____
(1393)	$x + 3 = 4$ _____	(1394)	$5 - x = 0$ _____
(1395)	$x - 4 = 5$ _____	(1396)	$x - 1 = 4$ _____
(1397)	$6 - x = 3$ _____	(1398)	$x + 7 = 10$ _____
(1399)	$7 + x = 11$ _____	(1400)	$3 - x = -6$ _____
(1401)	$9 + x = 18$ _____	(1402)	$3 - x = -4$ _____
(1403)	$6 + x = 8$ _____	(1404)	$8 + x = 14$ _____
(1405)	$1 - x = -3$ _____	(1406)	$x - 7 = -3$ _____
(1407)	$5 + x = 9$ _____	(1408)	$x + 1 = 7$ _____

Expressions - Single Step

Solve for the variable.

(1409) $x + 8 = 16$ _____

(1410) $x - 1 = 5$ _____

(1411) $1 + x = 2$ _____

(1412) $x - 2 = 0$ _____

(1413) $2 + x = 7$ _____

(1414) $x - 4 = 5$ _____

(1415) $x - 5 = -4$ _____

(1416) $x + 9 = 17$ _____

(1417) $9 + x = 13$ _____

(1418) $4 - x = -1$ _____

(1419) $9 - x = 6$ _____

(1420) $8 - x = 5$ _____

(1421) $x + 3 = 11$ _____

(1422) $7 + x = 15$ _____

(1423) $x + 5 = 13$ _____

(1424) $6 + x = 7$ _____

(1425) $x - 1 = 0$ _____

(1426) $3 - x = -1$ _____

(1427) $x + 5 = 11$ _____

(1428) $x + 7 = 10$ _____

Expressions - Single Step

Solve for the variable.

(1429) $x - 2 = 2$ _____

(1430) $x - 7 = 2$ _____

(1431) $x - 7 = 0$ _____

(1432) $6 + x = 12$ _____

(1433) $8 - x = 1$ _____

(1434) $4 - x = 1$ _____

(1435) $x - 5 = -2$ _____

(1436) $4 - x = -5$ _____

(1437) $x - 2 = 5$ _____

(1438) $x - 1 = 2$ _____

(1439) $x - 9 = -7$ _____

(1440) $x - 3 = 0$ _____

(1441) $x + 3 = 11$ _____

(1442) $9 + x = 16$ _____

(1443) $x - 4 = -2$ _____

(1444) $1 - x = -1$ _____

(1445) $x - 8 = 1$ _____

(1446) $4 + x = 6$ _____

(1447) $x - 7 = -3$ _____

(1448) $x - 2 = 7$ _____

Number Problems

Solve.

(1449) ____ Eleven less than a number is 23. Find the number.

(1450) ____ Two more than a number is 18. What is the number?

(1451) ____ Eighteen more than a number is 39. What is the number?

(1452) ____ A number increased by three is 11. Find the number.

(1453) ____ Two-thirds of a number is 18. Find the number.

(1454) ____ Five less than a number is 15. Find the number.

(1455) ____ The sum of a number and 30 is 39. Find the number.

(1456) ____ The sum of a number and seven is 17. Find the number.

(1457) ____ The sum of a number and 26 is 34. Find the number.

(1458) ____ A number diminished by 15 is 30. Find the number.

 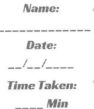 

Number Problems

Solve.

(1459) ____ Two-thirds of a number is 10. Find the number.

(1460) ____ One-third of a number is 8. Find the number.

(1461) ____ The sum of a number and 24 is 34. Find the number.

(1462) ____ Thirty more than a number is 33. What is the number?

(1463) ____ Twenty more than a number is 22. What is the number?

(1464) ____ A number diminished by 2 is 9. Find the number.

(1465) ____ The sum of a number and 23 is 34. Find the number.

(1466) ____ Eleven more than a number is 16. What is the number?

(1467) ____ A number increased by 26 is 32. Find the number.

(1468) ____ A number diminished by 19 is 9. Find the number.

Name:
_____
Date:
__/__/____
Time Taken:
____ Min

Number Problems

Solve.

(1469) ____ A number diminished by 7 is 23. Find the number.

(1470) ____ Nineteen more than a number is 21. What is the number?

(1471) ____ One-fifth of a number is 3. Find the number.

(1472) ____ One-half of a number is 2. Find the number.

(1473) ____ Two-fourths of a number is 12. Find the number.

(1474) ____ Twenty-six more than a number is 45. What is the number?

(1475) ____ A number increased by 18 is 21. Find the number.

(1476) ____ Twelve more than a number is 38. What is the number?

(1477) ____ A number decreased by 17 is 21. Find the number.

(1478) ____ Twenty-six less than a number is 6. Find the number.

Number Problems

Solve.

(1479) ____ A number decreased by 30 is 30. Find the number.

(1480) ____ A number increased by 15 is 31. Find the number.

(1481) ____ Twenty-eight less than a number is 4. Find the number.

(1482) ____ A number increased by nine is 20. Find the number.

(1483) ____ A number increased by 12 is 17. Find the number.

(1484) ____ A number increased by 11 is 33. Find the number.

(1485) ____ A number diminished by 25 is 19. Find the number.

(1486) ____ The sum of a number and 29 is 42. Find the number.

(1487) ____ A number increased by 22 is 31. Find the number.

(1488) ____ A number diminished by 18 is 27. Find the number.

Number Problems

Solve.

(1489) ____ A number increased by 21 is 39. Find the number.

(1490) ____ A number decreased by 21 is 25. Find the number.

(1491) ____ Two-fifths of a number is 6. Find the number.

(1492) ____ Two less than a number is 28. Find the number.

(1493) ____ One-half of a number is 5. Find the number.

(1494) ____ A number decreased by 25 is 12. Find the number.

(1495) ____ A number diminished by 12 is 8. Find the number.

(1496) ____ Three more than a number is 22. What is the number?

(1497) ____ The sum of a number and 23 is 31. Find the number.

(1498) ____ Two more than a number is 19. What is the number?

Fast Math Success Workbook Grade 5-6

126

Pre-Algebra Equations (One Step) Addition and Subtraction

Solve for the variable.

(1499) $x - 4 = 5$ _____

(1500) $22 - 4x = 6$ _____

(1501) $2 + x = 7$ _____

(1502) $1 + 5x = 41$ _____

(1503) $x - 3 = 5$ _____

(1504) $4 + x = 8$ _____

(1505) $6x + 8 = 50$ _____

(1506) $7x - 8 = 20$ _____

(1507) $5 - x = 1$ _____

(1508) $6 + 8x = 70$ _____

(1509) $7 - 2x = 1$ _____

(1510) $x - 2 = 7$ _____

(1511) $8 + 1x = 14$ _____

(1512) $4x + 9 = 21$ _____

(1513) $8x - 6 = 10$ _____

(1514) $27 - 3x = 3$ _____

(1515) $8 - x = 7$ _____

(1516) $4 + x = 7$ _____

(1517) $x + 3 = 12$ _____

(1518) $x - 2 = 1$ _____

Pre-Algebra Equations (One Step) Addition and Subtraction

Solve for the variable.

(1519) $2x - 4 = 0$ _____

(1520) $17 - 3x = 5$ _____

(1521) $2x - 1 = 17$ _____

(1522) $5x - 1 = 4$ _____

(1523) $7x - 1 = 34$ _____

(1524) $x - 5 = 3$ _____

(1525) $x + 3 = 9$ _____

(1526) $13 - 8x = 5$ _____

(1527) $3 + 5x = 18$ _____

(1528) $14 - 4x = 6$ _____

(1529) $2 + x = 6$ _____

(1530) $2x - 9 = 9$ _____

(1531) $x + 2 = 8$ _____

(1532) $3 - x = 1$ _____

(1533) $9x + 4 = 85$ _____

(1534) $8 - x = 6$ _____

(1535) $9 + 4x = 17$ _____

(1536) $4x + 8 = 20$ _____

(1537) $x + 5 = 9$ _____

(1538) $6x - 2 = 46$ _____

Pre-Algebra Equations (One Step) Addition and Subtraction

Solve for the variable.

(1539) $x + 8 = 9$ _____

(1540) $7 - x = 3$ _____

(1541) $2 + x = 6$ _____

(1542) $x + 6 = 12$ _____

(1543) $x - 5 = 2$ _____

(1544) $x + 9 = 13$ _____

(1545) $9x + 9 = 36$ _____

(1546) $5x - 4 = 31$ _____

(1547) $7 + 7x = 42$ _____

(1548) $x - 1 = 7$ _____

(1549) $x + 1 = 3$ _____

(1550) $18 - 5x = 3$ _____

(1551) $6x + 3 = 9$ _____

(1552) $1x + 9 = 18$ _____

(1553) $56 - 7x = 0$ _____

(1554) $7x + 4 = 18$ _____

(1555) $x + 9 = 16$ _____

(1556) $3x - 8 = 7$ _____

(1557) $4 - x = 1$ _____

(1558) $8x - 1 = 71$ _____

Pre-Algebra Equations (One Step) Addition and Subtraction

Solve for the variable.

(1559) $4x - 1 = 7$ _____

(1560) $x + 3 = 12$ _____

(1561) $29 - 3x = 8$ _____

(1562) $x + 4 = 5$ _____

(1563) $2 + x = 7$ _____

(1564) $x + 4 = 11$ _____

(1565) $x + 9 = 17$ _____

(1566) $3x + 6 = 27$ _____

(1567) $2x + 3 = 7$ _____

(1568) $x - 7 = 1$ _____

(1569) $9x + 2 = 83$ _____

(1570) $x + 1 = 4$ _____

(1571) $8 - x = 2$ _____

(1572) $9 - x = 3$ _____

(1573) $9x + 6 = 51$ _____

(1574) $x + 4 = 12$ _____

(1575) $9 + x = 18$ _____

(1576) $8 + 8x = 40$ _____

(1577) $8 + 1x = 17$ _____

(1578) $24 - 4x = 8$ _____

Pre-Algebra Equations (One Step) Addition and Subtraction

Solve for the variable.

(1579) $3 - x = 2$ _____

(1580) $48 - 5x = 8$ _____

(1581) $x + 3 = 10$ _____

(1582) $x + 2 = 11$ _____

(1583) $x + 4 = 8$ _____

(1584) $x + 1 = 9$ _____

(1585) $4x - 4 = 4$ _____

(1586) $8 - x = 6$ _____

(1587) $4 + x = 13$ _____

(1588) $3 + x = 9$ _____

(1589) $42 - 5x = 7$ _____

(1590) $x + 7 = 13$ _____

(1591) $9 + 2x = 17$ _____

(1592) $9x - 5 = 40$ _____

(1593) $7x + 3 = 59$ _____

(1594) $5 + 8x = 29$ _____

(1595) $4x + 6 = 22$ _____

(1596) $16 - 3x = 7$ _____

(1597) $11 - 2x = 3$ _____

(1598) $8 + x = 10$ _____

Name:

_ _ / _ _ / _ _ _ _

Date:

_ _ / _ _ / _ _ _ _

Time Taken:

_ _ _ _ Min

Pre-Algebra Equations (One Step) Multiplication and Division

Solve for the variable.

(1599) $x \div 3 = 4$ _____

(1600) $3x - 7 = 2$ _____

(1601) $49 - 6x = 7$ _____

(1602) $7 \times x = 7$ _____

(1603) $6x - 1 = 5$ _____

(1604) $4 + 6x = 34$ _____

(1605) $6x + 1 = 25$ _____

(1606) $x \div 5 = 5$ _____

(1607) $x \times 2 = 8$ _____

(1608) $3 \times x = 15$ _____

(1609) $x \times 8 = 8$ _____

(1610) $46 - 5x = 1$ _____

(1611) $8x - 8 = 16$ _____

(1612) $67 - 8x = 3$ _____

(1613) $x \times 5 = 45$ _____

(1614) $x \times 6 = 12$ _____

(1615) $x \times 6 = 24$ _____

(1616) $9x + 5 = 68$ _____

(1617) $43 - 5x = 8$ _____

(1618) $1 + 6x = 19$ _____

Fast Math Success Workbook Grade 5-6

132

Pre-Algebra Equations (One Step) Multiplication and Division

Solve for the variable.

(1619) $x \div 3 = 6$ _____

(1620) $x \times 1 = 8$ _____

(1621) $4x - 5 = 23$ _____

(1622) $6 \times x = 12$ _____

(1623) $8 \div x = 8$ _____

(1624) $3 \times x = 6$ _____

(1625) $14 \div x = 7$ _____

(1626) $4 \times x = 12$ _____

(1627) $45 \div x = 9$ _____

(1628) $8 \div x = 4$ _____

(1629) $3x - 2 = 16$ _____

(1630) $x \div 2 = 3$ _____

(1631) $x \div 2 = 1$ _____

(1632) $5x - 8 = 22$ _____

(1633) $30 \div x = 5$ _____

(1634) $6 + 2x = 8$ _____

(1635) $9x + 9 = 27$ _____

(1636) $x \times 1 = 3$ _____

(1637) $x \div 9 = 1$ _____

(1638) $7x - 7 = 42$ _____

Name:

Date:
__/__/____

Time Taken:
_____ Min

Pre-Algebra Equations (One Step) Multiplication and Division

Solve for the variable.

(1639) $x \div 2 = 3$ _____

(1640) $4x + 3 = 15$ _____

(1641) $4 \times x = 20$ _____

(1642) $2x - 8 = 2$ _____

(1643) $x \div 9 = 6$ _____

(1644) $5x - 4 = 6$ _____

(1645) $x \div 1 = 8$ _____

(1646) $32 \div x = 4$ _____

(1647) $6 + 1x = 13$ _____

(1648) $35 \div x = 7$ _____

(1649) $4x - 7 = 9$ _____

(1650) $2x - 6 = 4$ _____

(1651) $x \div 8 = 7$ _____

(1652) $6 \times x = 12$ _____

(1653) $5 + 2x = 17$ _____

(1654) $40 \div x = 5$ _____

(1655) $x \times 3 = 24$ _____

(1656) $4x - 7 = 1$ _____

(1657) $2 \times x = 12$ _____

(1658) $9 \times x = 9$ _____

Pre-Algebra Equations (One Step) Multiplication and Division

Solve for the variable.

(1659) $3x - 4 = 23$ _____

(1660) $9x - 7 = 74$ _____

(1661) $4 + 3x = 28$ _____

(1662) $5 + 5x = 25$ _____

(1663) $x \times 6 = 42$ _____

(1664) $2x - 1 = 5$ _____

(1665) $8x + 2 = 58$ _____

(1666) $4x - 8 = 16$ _____

(1667) $x \div 7 = 5$ _____

(1668) $12 \div x = 6$ _____

(1669) $7x + 8 = 22$ _____

(1670) $3 \times x = 27$ _____

(1671) $3 + 1x = 8$ _____

(1672) $x \times 4 = 16$ _____

(1673) $2 \div x = 2$ _____

(1674) $8x - 5 = 11$ _____

(1675) $28 - 7x = 0$ _____

(1676) $9 \times x = 72$ _____

(1677) $4 \div x = 4$ _____

(1678) $5 \times x = 5$ _____

Pre-Algebra Equations (One Step) Multiplication and Division

Solve for the variable.

(1679) $4x + 4 = 36$ _____

(1680) $14 \div x = 2$ _____

(1681) $18 \div x = 3$ _____

(1682) $x \times 4 = 20$ _____

(1683) $x \div 5 = 2$ _____

(1684) $9x + 7 = 34$ _____

(1685) $6x - 2 = 52$ _____

(1686) $27 - 9x = 9$ _____

(1687) $9x - 2 = 16$ _____

(1688) $1 + 5x = 16$ _____

(1689) $7x + 7 = 49$ _____

(1690) $3 + 6x = 45$ _____

(1691) $67 - 9x = 4$ _____

(1692) $1 \times x = 4$ _____

(1693) $x \div 6 = 2$ _____

(1694) $48 \div x = 6$ _____

(1695) $18 \div x = 6$ _____

(1696) $x \times 3 = 15$ _____

(1697) $1 + 7x = 50$ _____

(1698) $8 \times x = 16$ _____

Inequalities - Addition and Subtraction

Solve.

(1699) $x - 1 \le 6$

(1700) $x + 8 < 5$

(1701) $3 - x > 9$

(1702) $6 + x < 3$

(1703) $x + 8 \le 7$

(1704) $4 < x - 2$

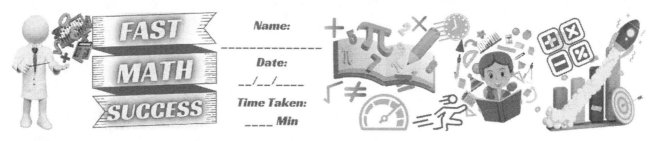

Inequalities - Addition and Subtraction

Solve.

(1705) $2 + x < 8$

(1706) $x - 1 > 5$

(1707) $2 - x < 3$

(1708) $x + 1 \geq 2$

(1709) $5 \geq 4 + x$

(1710) $8 < x - 2$

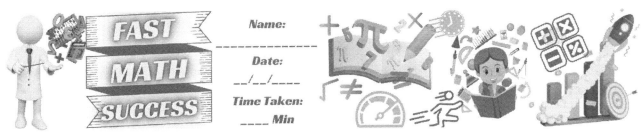

Inequalities - Addition and Subtraction

Solve.

(1711) $x - 7 \leq 8$

(1712) $5 \geq 5 + x$

(1713) $7 > x + 2$

(1714) $6 \geq 5 - x$

(1715) $6 < 4 - x$

(1716) $9 \geq 1 + x$

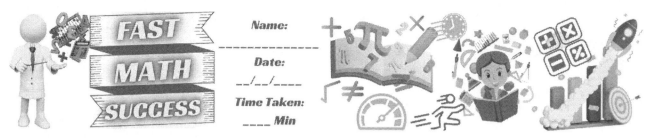

Inequalities - Multiplication and Division

Solve.

(1717) $2 > 6x$

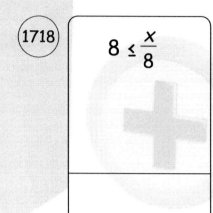

(1718) $8 \leq \dfrac{x}{8}$

(1719) $4 \geq 2x$

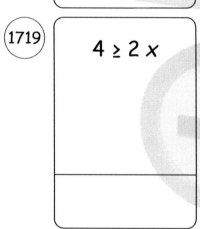

(1720) $6 \geq \dfrac{x}{2}$

(1721) $12 \geq 6x$

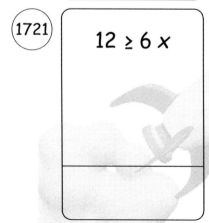

(1722) $\dfrac{x}{4} < 3$

Inequalities - Multiplication and Division

Solve.

(1723) $6x \leq 8$

(1724) $\dfrac{x}{8} \geq 6$

(1725) $4x \leq 3$

(1726) $\dfrac{x}{3} < 2$

(1727) $8 > \dfrac{x}{6}$

(1728) $15x > 9$

Inequalities - Multiplication and Division

Solve.

1729 $15\,x \le 12$

1730 $5 \ge \dfrac{x}{1}$

1731 $\dfrac{x}{6} \le 2$

1732 $6 < 18\,x$

1733 $\dfrac{x}{2} \le 7$

1734 $9 < 12\,x$

Find the Area and Perimeter

1735

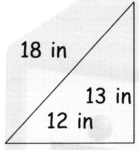

18 in

13 in

12 in

1736

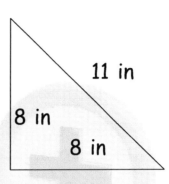

11 in

8 in

8 in

1737

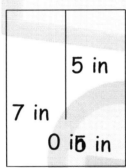

5 in

7 in

0 i5 in

1738

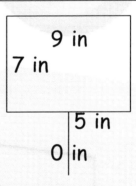

9 in

7 in

5 in

0 in

1739

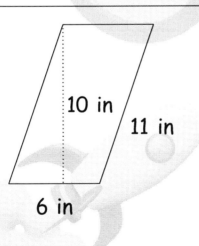

10 in

11 in

6 in

1740

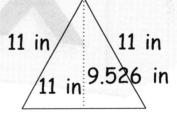

11 in   11 in

11 in 9.526 in

Find the Area and Perimeter

 (1741)

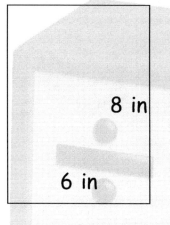

8 in

6 in

(1742)

12 in   6 in

5.60 in 13 in

(1743)

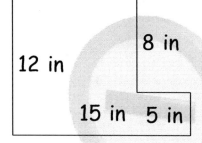

8 in

12 in

15 in   5 in

(1744)

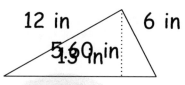

7 in

7 in

9 in

(1745)

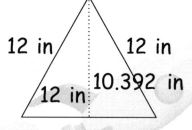

12 in   12 in

12 in   10.392 in

(1746)

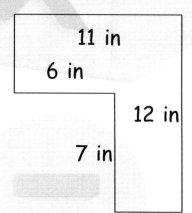

11 in

6 in

12 in

7 in

Name: _____

Date: ___/___/_____

Time Taken: ____ Min

Find the Area and Perimeter

 1747

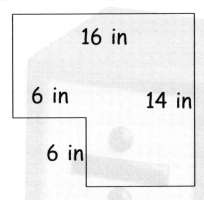

16 in

6 in

14 in

6 in

1748

15 in   15 in

13.75 in

12 in

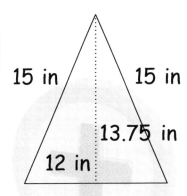

1749

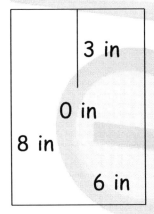

3 in

0 in

8 in

6 in

1750

15 in

17 in

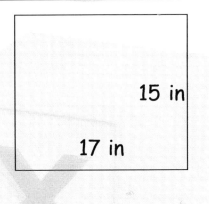

1751

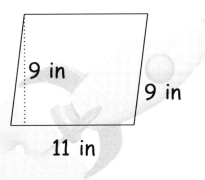

9 in

9 in

11 in

1752

2 in

5 in   0 in

8 in

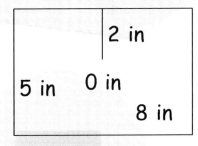

Find the Volume and Surface Area

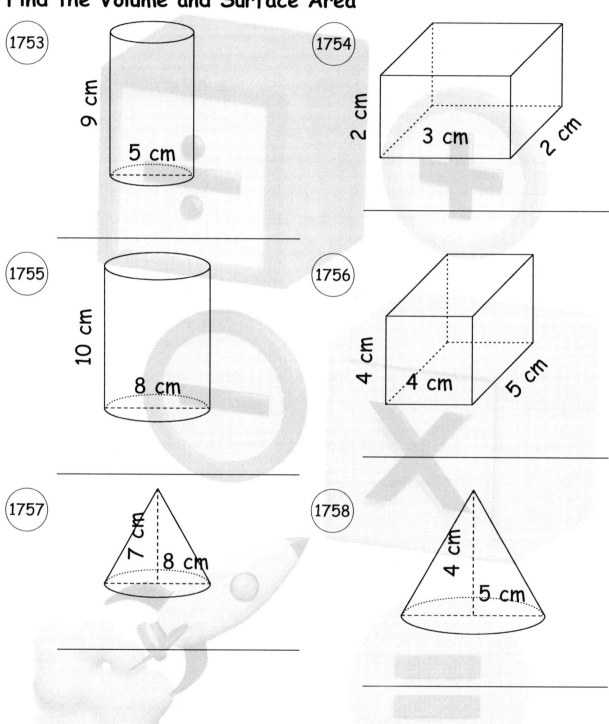

(1753) 9 cm 5 cm

(1754) 2 cm 3 cm 2 cm

(1755) 10 cm 8 cm

(1756) 4 cm 4 cm 5 cm

(1757) 7 cm 8 cm

(1758) 4 cm 5 cm

Find the Volume and Surface Area

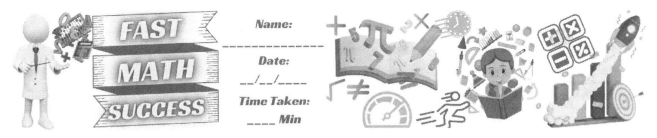

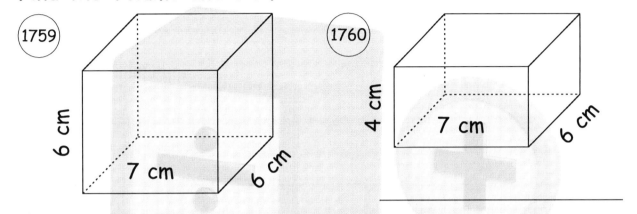

1759

6 cm
7 cm
6 cm

1760

4 cm
7 cm
6 cm

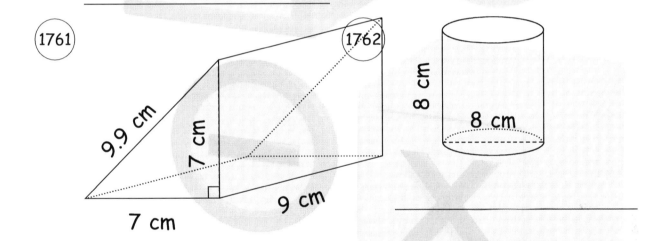

1761

9.9 cm
7 cm
7 cm
9 cm

1762

8 cm
8 cm

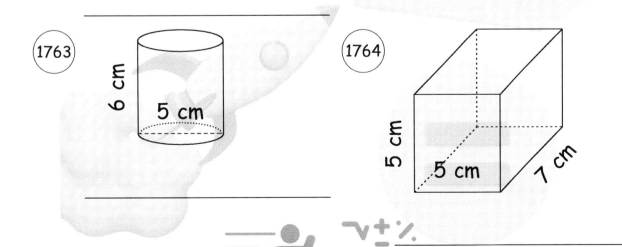

1763

6 cm
5 cm

1764

5 cm
5 cm
7 cm

Find the Volume and Surface Area

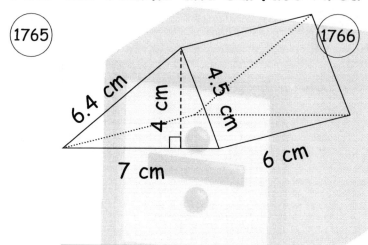

(1765)

6.4 cm 4 cm 4.5 cm 7 cm 6 cm

_____

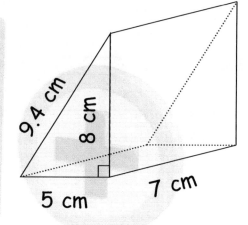

(1766)

9.4 cm 8 cm 5 cm 7 cm

_____

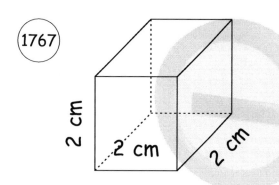

(1767)

2 cm 2 cm 2 cm

_____

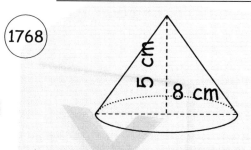

(1768)

5 cm 8 cm

_____

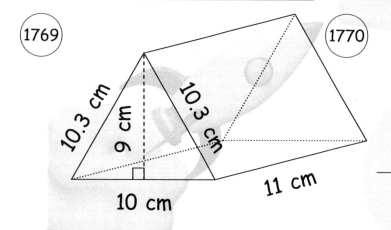

(1769)

10.3 cm 9 cm 10.3 cm 10 cm 11 cm

_____

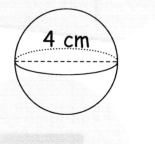

(1770)

4 cm

_____

Calculate the area of each circle.

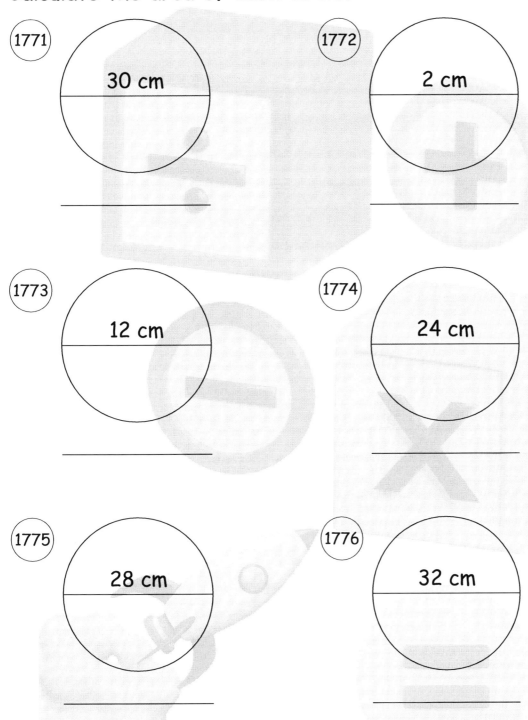

1771) 30 cm

1772) 2 cm

1773) 12 cm

1774) 24 cm

1775) 28 cm

1776) 32 cm

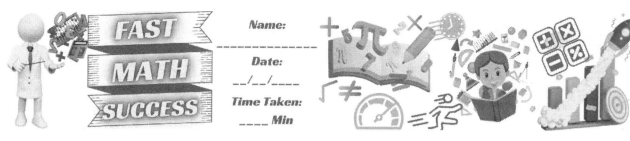
Calculate the area of each circle.

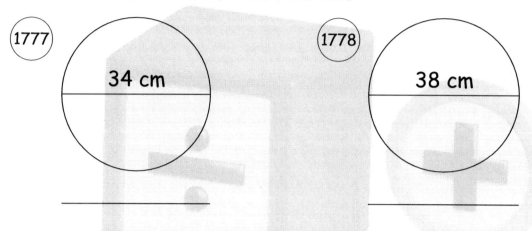

(1777)

34 cm

_____

(1778)

38 cm

_____

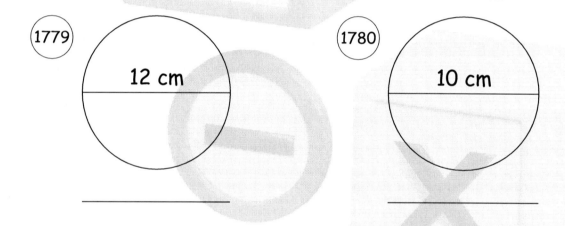

(1779)

12 cm

_____

(1780)

10 cm

_____

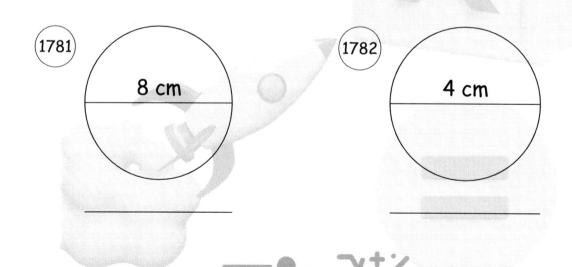

(1781)

8 cm

_____

(1782)

4 cm

_____

Calculate the area of each circle.

(1783) 40 cm

(1784) 8 cm

(1785) 24 cm

(1786) 20 cm

(1787) 32 cm

(1788) 36 cm

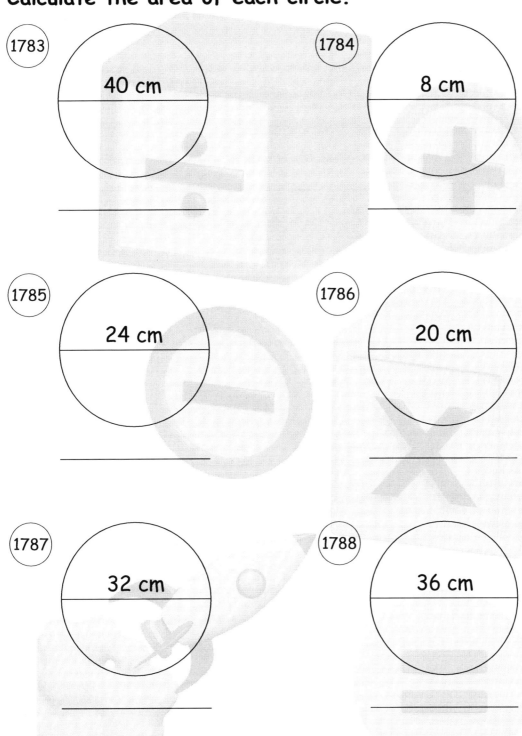

Calculate the circumference of each circle.

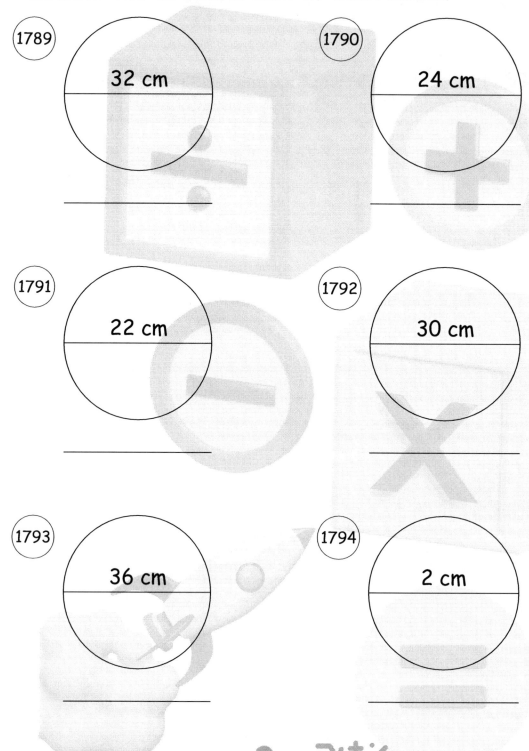

(1789)
32 cm

_____

(1790)
24 cm

_____

(1791)
22 cm

_____

(1792)
30 cm

_____

(1793)
36 cm

_____

(1794)
2 cm

_____

Calculate the circumference of each circle.

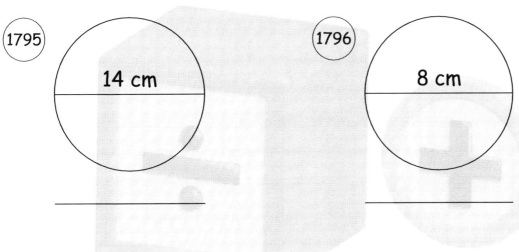

(1795)

14 cm

_____

(1796)

8 cm

_____

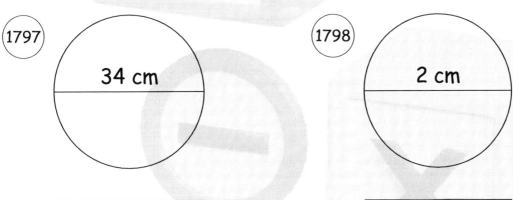

(1797)

34 cm

_____

(1798)

2 cm

_____

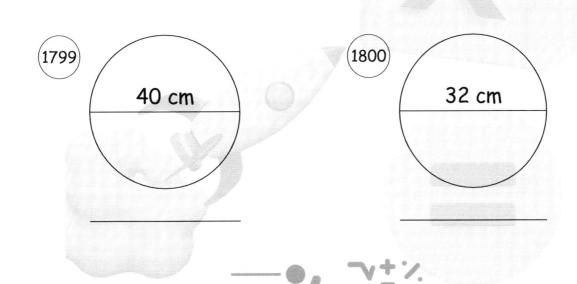

(1799)

40 cm

_____

(1800)

32 cm

_____

Calculate the circumference of each circle.

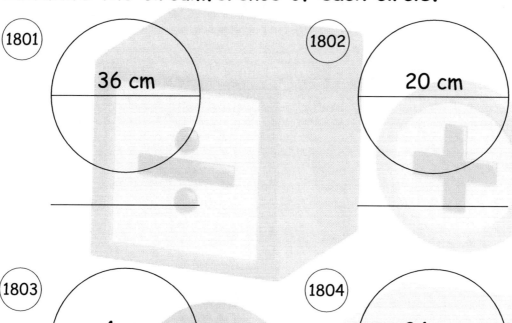

1801

36 cm

_____

1802

20 cm

_____

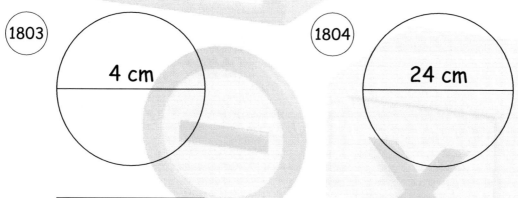

1803

4 cm

_____

1804

24 cm

_____

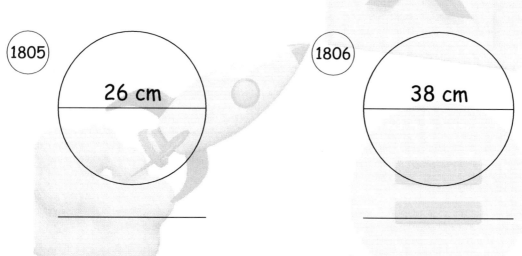

1805

26 cm

_____

1806

38 cm

_____

Measure of Center - Mean

Find the Mean of the following sets of data.

(1807) 53, 31, 9, 11, 48, 80, 80, 6

Mean = _____

(1808) 81, 85, 95, 13, 46, 5, 39, 7, 82

Mean = _____

(1809) 49, 10, 60, 81, 7, 52, 12, 34, 86

Mean = _____

(1810) 8, 40, 88, 24, 11, 81, 98, 26

Mean = _____

(1811) 87, 65, 59, 2, 60, 89, 19, 70, 75

Mean = _____

(1812) 84, 81, 67, 57, 39, 77

Mean = _____

Measure of Center - Mean

Find the Mean of the following sets of data.

(1813) 85, 36, 48, 21, 17, 8, 46, 78

Mean = _____

(1814) 96, 77, 62, 72, 41, 18, 57, 74, 15

Mean = _____

(1815) 15, 20, 17, 74, 48, 81

Mean = _____

(1816) 89, 20, 42, 11, 31, 68, 30, 66, 30

Mean = _____

(1817) 68, 62, 3, 88, 63, 60, 81, 19, 42

Mean = _____

(1818) 86, 62, 25, 98, 18, 78, 53, 18, 10

Mean = _____

Measure of Center - Median

Find the Median of the following sets of data.

(1819) 67, 53, 37, 22, 4, 37, 55, 59, 1

Median = ____

(1820) 75, 96, 15, 11, 67, 11, 32, 5

Median = ____

(1821) 78, 15, 69, 12, 54, 33

Median = ____

(1822) 1, 75, 87, 86, 56, 90, 3, 63, 58

Median = ____

(1823) 13, 58, 63, 14, 92, 46

Median = ____

(1824) 59, 66, 34, 5, 59, 7, 23, 27

Median = ____

Measure of Center - Median

Find the Median of the following sets of data.

(1825) 76, 95, 15, 66, 13, 1, 38, 49, 98

Median = ___

(1826) 13, 21, 36, 47, 16, 51, 98

Median = ___

(1827) 68, 97, 13, 39, 2, 52

Median = ___

(1828) 4, 97, 40, 59, 19, 48, 35

Median = ___

(1829) 8, 95, 27, 78, 49, 11, 90

Median = ___

(1830) 42, 25, 90, 63, 20, 64, 60

Median = ___

Name:
_____
Date:
___/___/_____
Time Taken:
_____ Min

Measure of Center - Mode

Find the Mode of the following sets of data.

(1831) 51, 92, 56, 99, 43, 16, 35, 36

Mode = _____

(1832) 61, 94, 84, 25, 25, 91, 17

Mode = _____

(1833) 26, 54, 81, 90, 14, 90

Mode = _____

(1834) 18, 94, 58, 97, 5, 60, 56, 44, 8

Mode = _____

(1835) 49, 19, 38, 91, 53, 5, 84, 60, 75

Mode = _____

(1836) 33, 1, 71, 34, 33, 94, 24, 86

Mode = _____

Name:

Date:
__/__/____

Time Taken:
___.___ Min

Measure of Center - Mode

Find the Mode of the following sets of data.

(1837) 98, 25, 98, 37, 81, 30, 50, 70, 34

Mode = ____

(1838) 98, 98, 2, 39, 55, 78, 92, 54, 45

Mode = ____

(1839) 65, 86, 34, 39, 13, 42, 94, 7

Mode = ____

(1840) 57, 14, 20, 83, 62, 64, 74, 19, 61

Mode = ____

(1841) 32, 45, 71, 68, 88, 88, 22

Mode = ____

(1842) 20, 7, 86, 59, 37, 77

Mode = ____

Measure of Variability - Range
Find the Range of the following sets of data.

(1843) 22, 78, 80, 87, 29, 38, 53, 60

Range = ____

(1844) 13, 56, 42, 75, 73, 37, 50, 50

Range = ____

(1845) 36, 35, 28, 20, 94, 47, 48, 82

Range = ____

(1846) 76, 76, 98, 13, 20, 6

Range = ____

(1847) 56, 36, 70, 79, 92, 41, 4

Range = ____

(1848) 74, 35, 36, 65, 1, 19, 88, 29, 93

Range = ____

Measure of Variability - Range

Find the Range of the following sets of data.

(1849) 16, 51, 71, 69, 70, 51, 31

Range = ____

(1850) 17, 83, 74, 31, 97, 12

Range = ____

(1851) 52, 39, 41, 41, 7, 1

Range = ____

(1852) 7, 5, 93, 44, 10, 46, 62, 99

Range = ____

(1853) 91, 55, 93, 29, 59, 54, 83, 60, 47

Range = ____

(1854) 41, 50, 36, 5, 5, 53, 96

Range = ____

Name:
_ _ _ _ _ _ _ _ _ _ _ _ _ _

Date:
__/__/____

Time Taken:
_ _ _ _ Min

ANSWERS

Page 1: Pre-Algebra - Order of Operations (PEMDAS)
1. -84   2. 1,581   3. 1.9   4. 11   5. 3,717   6. -25   7. 1.2
8. 23   9. -602   10. 59

Page 2: Pre-Algebra - Order of Operations (PEMDAS)
11. 11,130   12. 12,089   13. 1,820   14. 222   15. 5,607   16. 11,880
17. 1,380   18. 2,037   19. 33   20. 2

Page 3: Pre-Algebra - Order of Operations (PEMDAS)
21. 7,362   22. 217   23. 111   24. 136   25. 1,701   26. 227
27. 3,958   28. -94   29. 536   30. 786

Page 4: Pre-Algebra - Order of Operations (PEMDAS)
31. 1,196   32. 135   33. 67   34. 48   35. 1,456   36. -101
37. 4   38. 18,864   39. 106   40. 101

Page 5: Pre-Algebra - Order of Operations (PEMDAS)
41. 1,820   42. 75   43. 1.3   44. 55   45. 1,406   46. 10
47. 12,126   48. 150   49. 1,811   50. 12,177

Page 6: Pre-Algebra - Order of Operations (PEMDAS)
51. -19   52. 49   53. 1,890   54. 4,620   55. 7,579   56. 160
57. 30   58. 0.5   59. 7   60. 56

Page 7: Pre-Algebra - Order of Operations (PEMDAS)
61. 1,496   62. 6,048   63. -51   64. -212   65. 714   66. -73
67. -78   68. -93   69. 2.2   70. 1,471

Page 8: Pre-Algebra - Order of Operations (PEMDAS)
71. 121   72. 44   73. 232   74. 172   75. 1,935   76. 3,844
77. 236   78. 206   79. 85   80. 124

Page 9: Fractions Addition - Unlike Denominator
81. 178/99   82. 200/171   83. 11/15   84. 69/55   85. 103/126

86. **219/200**   87. **11/8**   88. **57/40**   89. **223/180**   90. **85/184**

Page 10:   Fractions Addition - Unlike Denominator
91. **9/10**   92. **11/28**   93. **108/95**   94. **17/14**   95. **23/18**

96. **361/280**   97. **17/20**   98. **4/5**   99. **23/16**   100. **83/88**

Page 11:   Fractions Addition - Unlike Denominator
101. **5/4**   102. **1149/1100**   103. **23/20**   104. **128/91**

105. **10/21**   106. **431/280**   107. **43/40**   108. **537/736**

109. **449/600**   110. **193/112**

Page 12:   Fractions Addition - Unlike Denominator
111. **109/130**   112. **37/50**   113. **84/85**   114. **515/456**   115. **227/130**

116. **61/50**   117. **619/330**   118. **1/1**   119. **61/36**   120. **43/30**

Page 13:   Fractions Addition - Unlike Denominator
121. **25/42**   122. **69/190**   123. **226/165**   124. **33/28**   125. **11/15**

126. **257/150**   127. **21/16**   128. **5/6**   129. **7/6**   130. **53/36**

Page 14:   Fractions Subtraction - Unlike Denominator
131. **153/266**   132. **89/400**   133. **1/6**   134. **95/357**   135. **2/15**

136. **5/14**   137. **2/9**   138. **27/286**   139. **34/165**   140. **1/5**

Page 15:   Fractions Subtraction - Unlike Denominator
141. **1/3**   142. **9/143**   143. **3/50**   144. **23/48**   145. **183/760**

146. **1/6**   147. **11/76**   148. **37/80**   149. **29/385**   150. **29/75**

Page 16:   Fractions Subtraction - Unlike Denominator
151. **1/20**   152. **2/3**   153. **1/20**   154. **5/12**   155. **1/6**   156. **2/5**

157. **1/24**   158. **7/30**   159. **1/4**   160. **7/15**

Page 17:   Fractions Subtraction - Unlike Denominator
161. **69/100**   162. **5/12**   163. **25/44**   164. **7/25**   165. **17/275**

166. **19/138**   167. **1/2**   168. **1017150**   169. **17/90**   170. **205/266**

Page 18: Fractions Subtraction - Unlike Denominator

171. 1/30

172. **51/176**

173. **7/110**

174. **89/168**

175. **1/5**

176. **97/1100**

177. **4/15**

178. **353/1275**

179. **2/15**

180. **13/30**

Page 19: Fractions Multiplication

181. **49/99**

182. **7/18**

183. **5/72**

184. **26/165**

185. **3/10**

186. **2/5**

187. **1/26**

188. **119/225**

189. **8/27**

190. **5/57**

191. **7/80**

192. **1/2**

193. **1/8**

194. **1083/1400**

195. **247/400**

196. **5/24**

197. **14/33**

198. **49/143**

199. **1/4**

200. **57/175**

Page 20: Fractions Multiplication

201. **25/48**

202. **697/3000**

203. **14/95**

204. **3/10**

205. **7/30**

206. **3/22**

207. **63/368**

208. **21/100**

209. **2/175**

210. **11/36**

211. **145/672**

212. **11/30**

213. **36/125**

214. **8/21**

215. **25/88**

216. **11/80**

217. **2/25**

218. **3/26**

219. **27/176**

220. **22/75**

Page 21: Fractions Multiplication

221. **1/6**

222. **7/100**

223. **49/900**

224. **2/17**

225. **87/280**

226. **9/25**

227. **17/56**

228. **13/24**

229. **19/100**

230. **2747/4200**

231. **6/115**

232. **44/125**

233. **2/19**

234. **7/450**

235. **33/200**

236. **1/25**

237. **16/27**

238. **9/22**

239. **1/15**

240. **2/11**

Page 22: Fractions Division

241. **32/7**

242. **11/5**

243. **45/56**

244. **10/1**

245. **66/35**

246. **17/14**

247. **9/7**

248. **12/13**

249. **59/50**

250. **165/152**

Page 23: Fractions Division

251. **200/23**   252. **15/28**   253. **1/4**   254. **17/169**   255. **8/9**

256. **19/20**   257. **45/4**   258. **9/7**   259. **75/98**   260. **540/713**

Page 24: Fractions Division

261. **220/51**   262. **288/175**   263. **17/6**   264. **2/1**   265. **2/1**

266. **50/21**   267. **11/19**   268. **112/33**   269. **51/8**   270. **50/147**

Page 25: Multiplication with Whole Numbers

271. **2**   272. **1/5**   273. **3 1/2**   274. **4/5**   275. **1/4**   276. **1/2**

277. **4 2/3**   278. **5/8**   279. **2 2/3**   280. **1 2/3**   281. **1 3/5**   282. **4 1/2**

283. **2/3**   284. **1/3**   285. **5/8**   286. **1 1/2**   287. **1 1/5**   288. **2**

289. **1 1/2**   290. **2/3**

Page 26: Multiplication with Whole Numbers

291. **3/4**   292. **3 1/2**   293. **5 1/4**   294. **6 3/4**   295. **3**   296. **3**

297. **2/3**   298. **1/2**   299. **3**   300. **1 1/2**   301. **3/5**   302. **1 1/4**

303. **2/3**   304. **1/2**   305. **1 1/2**   306. **6**   307. **3 1/5**   308. **2/3**

309. **5/8**   310. **3 1/5**

Page 27: Multiplication with Whole Numbers

311. **1 1/2**   312. **4**   313. **1/6**   314. **4 2/3**   315. **1 1/5**   316. **3/4**

317. **1/4**   318. **3 3/4**   319. **2/3**   320. **5 2/5**   321. **4 2/3**   322. **1 3/4**

323. **1 1/6**   324. **2**   325. **7 1/5**   326. **5 1/4**   327. **1/6**   328. **1 3/4**

329. **2/5**   330. **1/4**

Page 28: Division with Whole Numbers

331. **1/4**   332. **2/3**   333. **5/12**   334. **1/36**   335. **1/5**   336. **3/20**

337. **1/9**   338. **1/18**   339. **1/54**   340. **3/16**   341. **4/25**   342. **1/12**

343. **5/6**   344. **5/24**   345. **3/16**   346. **4/35**   347. **1/4**   348. **3/40**

349. **1/24**   350. **2/21**

Page 29:   Division with Whole Numbers

351. **1/6**   352. **7/64**   353. **1/45**   354. **1/24**   355. **1/4**   356. **1/12**

357. **1/12**   358. **1/20**   359. **1/12**   360. **1/40**   361. **1/18**   362. **1/18**

363. **5/72**   364. **1/20**   365. **2/9**   366. **3/35**   367. **1/4**   368. **3/16**

369. **5/6**   370. **1/18**

Page 30:   Division with Whole Numbers

371. **1/24**   372. **2/15**   373. **1/6**   374. **3/10**   375. **1/45**   376. **3/56**

377. **1/10**   378. **1/6**   379. **1/27**   380. **1/3**   381. **1/18**   382. **1/16**

383. **1/12**   384. **4/35**   385. **3/8**   386. **5/24**   387. **1/10**   388. **1/18**

389. **1/24**   390. **1/8**

Page 31:   Mixed Fractions - Multiplication

391. **29 23/144**   392. **30 66/133**   393. **28 19/32**   394. **30 17/99**

395. **46 7/30**   396. **39 2/17**   397. **14 13/14**   398. **72 25/48**

399. **16 73/75**   400. **21 4/25**

Page 32:   Mixed Fractions - Multiplication

401. **50 343/540**   402. **15 40/99**   403. **28 52/105**   404. **19 53/80**

405. **3 31/46**   406. **53 93/238**   407. **12 3/10**   408. **19 41/76**

409. **6 47/54**   410. **24 269/440**

Page 33:   Mixed Fractions - Multiplication

411. **4 14/19**   412. **29 101/105**   413. **46 2/3**

414. **13 509/720**   415. **8 111/112**   416. **55 13/19**

417. **7 14/25**   418. **30 10/11**   419. **20 637/1200**

420. **7 7/20**

Page 34:   Mixed Fractions- Division

421. **1 3/140**   422. **50/57**   423. **3 27/49**

424. **1 3629/7371**   425. **5 11/20**   426. **1 55/441**

Name:

Date:
__/__/____

Time Taken:
___.___ Min

427. **46/121**

428. **2 223/550**

429. **95/136**

430. **99/466**

Page 35:   Mixed Fractions- Division

431. **400/1467**

432. **3525/3983**

433. **45/88**

434. **1 647/1368**

435. **99/160**

436. **1 1709/2355**

437. **251/340**

438. **341/540**

439. **342/365**

440. **1 289/308**

Page 36:   Mixed Fractions- Division

441. **1329/1700**

442. **2 16/125**

443. **1 1219/2640**

444. **23/70**

445. **434/1875**

446. **1155/1376**

447. **132/497**

448. **5 29/221**

449. **3 1203/1424**

450. **2 74/357**

Page 37:   Fractions: Multiple Operations

451. **1**

452. **2/3**

453. **7/8**

454. **2/3**

455. **1 1/2**

456. **1 1/4**

457. **1/6**

458. **2/27**

459. **13/20**

460. **147/512**

Page 38:   Fractions: Multiple Operations

461. **1 11/16**

462. **19/25**

463. **24/125**

464. **1/5**

465. **43/80**

466. **4/27**

467. **1/4**

468. **1/4**

469. **19/24**

470. **2/5**

Page 39:   Fractions: Multiple Operations

471. **1 1/2**

472. **2**

473. **27/80**

474. **1 1/5**

475. **1 2/3**

476. **2**

477. **0**

478. **1 2/5**

479. **1 5/6**

480. **1 7/8**

Page 40:   Fractions: Multiple Operations

481. **5/6**

482. **47/48**

483. **3**

484. **1 1/10**

485. **2/9**

486. **7/30**

487. **8/9**

488. **3/8**

489. **2/3**

490. **1 1/3**

Page 41:   Fractions: Multiple Operations

491. **1 1/15**

492. **4**

493. **1 1/2**

494. **1/6**

495. **0**

496. **3 11/15**   497. **5/216**   498. **5/216**   499. **1/8**   500. **10**

Page 42:   Fractions: Multiple Operations

501. **1 11/20**   502. **1/2**   503. **4**   504. **6 7/8**   505. **7/8**

506. **9 7/15**   507. **2/5**   508. **13/18**   509. **2 1/4**   510. **-1/10**

Page 43:   Fractions: Multiple Operations

511. **-1/4**   512. **3 1/2**   513. **3/512**   514. **2/27**   515. **5/512**

516. **1/3**   517. **8/9**   518. **13/16**   519. **12/25**   520. **48/125**

Page 44:   Fractions: Multiple Operations

521. **1 2/5**   522. **1 1/8**   523. **19/24**   524. **24/25**   525. **5/6**   526. **4**

527. **1 4/5**   528. **3/5**   529. **1/3**   530. **1/4**

Page 45:   Fractions: Multiple Operations

531. **13/48**   532. **8 1/3**   533. **11/36**   534. **4/15**   535. **2 6/25**

536. **2**   537. **1/216**   538. **12/125**   539. **1/9**   540. **1 3/4**

Page 46:   Simplifying Fractions

541. **6**   542. **5 1/3**   543. **6 3/5**   544. **4 9/14**   545. **8 1/3**

546. **3 3/5**   547. **2/3**   548. **5 1/8**   549. **8**   550. **8**

551. **2/3**   552. **8 3/4**   553. **5 3/4**   554. **7 1/6**   555. **7 9/10**

556. **9**   557. **7**   558. **2**   559. **8**   560. **1/7**

Page 47:   Simplifying Fractions

561. **1/2**   562. **5**   563. **9**   564. **5**   565. **3 13/14**

566. **2**   567. **2/3**   568. **6**   569. **1/5**   570. **3 1/3**

571. **1/4**   572. **9/10**   573. **4 13/14**   574. **2 5/6**   575. **3 1/2**

576. **2**   577. **8 7/15**   578. **2**   579. **1/8**   580. **5/6**

Page 48:   Simplifying Fractions

581. **9 1/2**   582. **1/5**   583. **5 14/15**   584. **6**   585. **4 1/4**

586. **3/5**   587. **2/3**   588. **2**   589. **6 3/4**   590. **3/4**

Name:

Date:
__/__/____

Time Taken:
___.___ Min

591. **7 3/7**   592. **2**   593. **1/5**   594. **2**   595. **6 3/4**

596. **8 3/7**   597. **3 1/6**   598. **3**   599. **2 1/4**   600. **6**

Page 49:   Simplifying Fractions

601. **4**   602. **5**   603. **9 1/2**   604. **2**   605. **8 1/3**

606. **8 1/3**   607. **4**   608. **1/12**   609. **1/14**   610. **5/8**

611. **6 3/5**   612. **1/2**   613. **3/5**   614. **5/12**   615. **5 2/3**

616. **2 1/4**   617. **6/7**   618. **5 1/5**   619. **9 1/3**   620. **3 9/10**

Page 50:   Simplifying Fractions

621. **7**   622. **5/7**   623. **6 5/6**   624. **5 5/6**   625. **5**

626. **3 1/4**   627. **4**   628. **9/10**   629. **9**   630. **7/8**

631. **3 1/3**   632. **3/5**   633. **1/3**   634. **7 1/14**   635. **8**

636. **3 1/2**   637. **4**   638. **3**   639. **1/2**   640. **9 1/3**

Page 51:   Associative Property

641. **1, 7**   642. **2, 6**   643. **8, 7**   644. **6, 3**   645. **5, 2**   646. **6, 7**   647. **1, 9**

648. **3, 7**   649. **4, 2**   650. **2, 9**   651. **9, 3**   652. **5, 2**

Page 52:   Associative Property

653. **4, 3**   654. **3, 7**   655. **4, 8**   656. **5, 8**   657. **9, 7**   658. **8, 7**   659. **5, 7**

660. **4, 3**   661. **5, 4**   662. **1, 6**   663. **6, 2**   664. **7, 8**

Page 53:   Associative Property

665. **6, 8**   666. **3, 6**   667. **8, 4**   668. **2, 6**   669. **3, 8**   670. **8, 1**   671. **4, 7**

672. **6, 7**   673. **2, 7**   674. **2, 7**   675. **3, 6**   676. **2, 9**

Page 54:   Commutative Property

677. **7**   678. **1**   679. **6**   680. **8**   681. **6**   682. **5**   683. **8**   684. **1**   685. **7**   686. **5**

687. **6**   688. **3**   689. **1**   690. **2**   691. **4**   692. **4**   693. **7**   694. **5**   695. **1**   696. **7**

697. **2**   698. **6**

Fast Math Success Workbook Grade 5-6

170

Page 55: Commutative Property

699. **8**   700. **5**   701. **8**   702. **2**   703. **2**   704. **2**   705. **2**   706. **6**   707. **3**   708. **8**

709. **1**   710. **7**   711. **5**   712. **8**   713. **7**   714. **9**   715. **6**   716. **5**   717. **4**   718. **5**

719. **3**   720. **4**

Page 56: Commutative Property

721. **5**   722. **1**   723. **3**   724. **2**   725. **9**   726. **1**   727. **4**   728. **4**   729. **9**   730. **4**

731. **3**   732. **8**   733. **2**   734. **2**   735. **8**   736. **2**   737. **6**   738. **4**   739. **4**   740. **9**

741. **7**   742. **3**

Page 57: Distributive Property

743. **8, 2**   744. **2, 1**   745. **1, 3**   746. **6, 1**   747. **2, 1**   748. **3, 8**   749. **6, 7**

750. **8, 4**   751. **2, 1**   752. **7, 1**   753. **3, 5**   754. **8, 7**

Page 58: Distributive Property

755. **4, 8**   756. **9, 4**   757. **6, 3**   758. **4, 2**   759. **2, 3**   760. **6, 8**   761. **7, 4**

762. **8, 6**   763. **5, 7**   764. **2, 8**   765. **8, 4**   766. **4, 7**

Page 59: Distributive Property

767. **7, 2**   768. **9, 4**   769. **8, 2**   770. **2, 7**   771. **9, 5**   772. **5, 3**   773. **4, 8**

774. **6, 8**   775. **7, 1**   776. **4, 7**   777. **5, 4**   778. **4, 7**

Page 60: Percent

779. **400**   780. **2%**   781. **349**   782. **861**   783. **33**

784. **488**   785. **282**   786. **306**   787. **135.75**   788. **10%**

789. **2%**   790. **5%**   791. **207**   792. **470**   793. **461**

794. **25%**   795. **10%**   796. **2%**   797. **297**   798. **20%**

Page 61: Percent

799. **10%**   800. **472**   801. **21.15**   802. **827**   803. **22.8**   804. **9.85**

805. **69**   806. **193.4**   807. **162**   808. **25%**   809. **8%**   810. **15.6**

811. **464**   812. **582**   813. **12.9**   814. **432**   815. **25%**   816. **158.4**

Name:

Date:
__/__/____

Time Taken:
___ __ Min

817. **804**   818. **36.56**

Page 62:   Percent

819. **20%**   820. **8%**   821. **39.2**   822. **2%**   823. **38.3**

824. **597**   825. **8%**   826. **10%**   827. **143.25**   828. **17**

829. **135**   830. **32.45**   831. **123.6**   832. **847**   833. **20%**

834. **32.1**   835. **25%**   836. **17.1**   837. **56.64**   838. **25.95**

Page 63:   Percent

839. **104**   840. **21.4**   841. **23**   842. **2.55**   843. **20%**   844. **8%**

845. **396**   846. **64.2**   847. **74**   848. **2%**   849. **5%**   850. **212**

851. **14.32**   852. **62.3**   853. **178**   854. **2%**   855. **4.3**   856. **908**

857. **816**   858. **793**

Page 64:   Percent

859. **550**   860. **134.75**   861. **21.75**   862. **14.8**   863. **2%**

864. **10%**   865. **8%**   866. **65.5**   867. **433**   868. **27.6**

869. **2%**   870. **20%**   871. **15%**   872. **725**   873. **10%**

874. **206**   875. **216**   876. **21.6**   877. **58.24**   878. **119**

Page 65:   Percent and Decimals

879. **0.07**   880. **0.71**   881. **0.72**   882. **0.69**   883. **0.03**   884. **0.73**

885. **0.37**   886. **0.32**   887. **0.44**   888. **0.41**   889. **0.24**   890. **0.49**

891. **0.79**   892. **0.58**   893. **0.14**   894. **0.06**   895. **0.91**   896. **0.67**

897. **0.83**   898. **0.16**

Page 66:   Percent and Decimals

899. **0.03**   900. **0.22**   901. **0.66**   902. **0.78**   903. **0.65**   904. **0.01**

905. **0.13**   906. **0.67**   907. **0.74**   908. **0.25**   909. **0.87**   910. **0.85**

911. **0.06**   912. **0.07**   913. **0.81**   914. **0.61**   915. **0.77**   916. **0.19**

917. **0.18**   918. **0.52**

Page 67: **Percent and Decimals**

919. **79%**   920. **42%**   921. **2%**   922. **86%**   923. **98%**   924. **50%**   925. **40%**

926. **99%**   927. **54%**   928. **17%**   929. **52%**   930. **75%**   931. **24%**   932. **19%**

933. **31%**   934. **30%**   935. **95%**   936. **73%**   937. **49%**   938. **43%**

Page 68: **Percent and Decimals**

939. **19%**   940. **75%**   941. **13%**   942. **58%**   943. **17%**   944. **23%**   945. **14%**

946. **30%**   947. **74%**   948. **61%**   949. **22%**   950. **91%**   951. **79%**   952. **88%**

953. **7%**   954. **76%**   955. **69%**   956. **28%**   957. **92%**   958. **98%**

Page 69: **Percent and Decimals**

959. **98%**   960. **14%**   961. **7%**   962. **21%**   963. **13%**   964. **38%**   965. **80%**

966. **68%**   967. **48%**   968. **90%**   969. **36%**   970. **23%**   971. **28%**   972. **74%**

973. **40%**   974. **33%**   975. **17%**   976. **86%**   977. **24%**   978. **43%**

Page 70: **Percent and Decimals**

979. **91%**   980. **53%**   981. **34%**   982. **41%**   983. **43%**   984. **7%**   985. **81%**

986. **5%**   987. **21%**   988. **52%**   989. **22%**   990. **78%**   991. **99%**   992. **51%**

993. **96%**   994. **11%**   995. **76%**   996. **6%**   997. **48%**   998. **74%**

Page 71: **Percent - Advanced**

999. **71**   1000. **730**   1001. **9.8%**   1002. **51**   1003. **6**

1004. **7.2%**   1005. **4.203**   1006. **940**   1007. **0.476**   1008. **0.2%**

1009. **4.484**   1010. **0.435**   1011. **5.0%**   1012. **9.2%**   1013. **1.445**

1014. **2.5%**   1015. **8**   1016. **3**   1017. **56**   1018. **8.5%**

Page 72: **Percent - Advanced**

1019. **0.035**   1020. **0.004**   1021. **0.016**   1022. **0.904**   1023. **0.8%**

1024. **0.208**   1025. **67**   1026. **1.1%**   1027. **6**   1028. **0.055**

1029. **7.7%**   1030. **0.102**   1031. **3**   1032. **0.3%**   1033. **9.1%**

1034. **622**   1035. **38**   1036. **8.8%**   1037. **14.269**   1038. **0.9%**

Page 73:   Percent - Advanced

1039. **775**	1040. **249**	1041. **86**	1042. **9**	1043. **0.203**
1044. **0.006**	1045. **51**	1046. **89.73**	1047. **2.501**	1048. **3.6%**
1049. **0.6%**	1050. **0.384**	1051. **0.1%**	1052. **414**	1053. **87**
1054. **0.2%**	1055. **0.3%**	1056. **6**	1057. **91**	1058. **30**

Page 74:   Percent - Advanced

1059. **3**	1060. **0.3%**	1061. **1.7%**	1062. **0.2%**	1063. **77**
1064. **12.673**	1065. **38**	1066. **42**	1067. **836**	1068. **48**
1069. **28.497**	1070. **0.165**	1071. **0.696**	1072. **7**	1073. **1.4%**
1074. **71**	1075. **31**	1076. **2**	1077. **679**	1078. **75**

Page 75:   Percent - Advanced

1079. **20.24**	1080. **5.7%**	1081. **67**	1082. **745**	1083. **0.4%**
1084. **7.4%**	1085. **972**	1086. **24.056**	1087. **2**	1088. **3.3%**
1089. **3**	1090. **4.912**	1091. **2**	1092. **50**	1093. **59.85**
1094. **0.342**	1095. **10.008**	1096. **90**	1097. **0.012**	1098. **0.012**

Page 76:   Ratio Conversions

1099.

	Ratio	Fraction	Percent	Decimal
a.	3:3	3/3	100%	1
b.	2:7	2/7	28.6%	0.286
c.	1:10	1/10	10%	0.1
d.	2:5	2/5	40%	0.4
e.	2:4	2/4	50%	0.5
f.	2:10	2/10	20%	0.2
g.	5:7	5/7	71.4%	0.714
h.	1:8	1/8	12.5%	0.125
i.	3:5	3/5	60%	0.6
j.	1:2	1/2	50%	0.5
k.	4:7	4/7	57.1%	0.571
l.	2:9	2/9	22.2%	0.222
m.	5:6	5/6	83.3%	0.833

Page 77:   Ratio Conversions

1100.

	Ratio	Fraction	Percent	Decimal
a.	4:5	4/5	80%	0.8
b.	2:2	2/2	100%	1
c.	4:9	4/9	44.4%	0.444
d.	2:10	2/10	20%	0.2
e.	3:5	3/5	60%	0.6
f.	6:8	6/8	75%	0.75
g.	1:3	1/3	33.3%	0.333
h.	2:6	2/6	33.3%	0.333
i.	4:7	4/7	57.1%	0.571
j.	5:8	5/8	62.5%	0.625
k.	3:9	3/9	33.3%	0.333
l.	5:10	5/10	50%	0.5
m.	4:10	4/10	40%	0.4

Page 78:   Ratio Conversions

1101.

	Ratio	Fraction	Percent	Decimal
a.	5:8	5/8	62.5%	0.625
b.	5:9	5/9	55.6%	0.556
c.	1:1	1/1	100%	1
d.	5:10	5/10	50%	0.5
e.	2:7	2/7	28.6%	0.286
f.	7:8	7/8	87.5%	0.875
g.	5:6	5/6	83.3%	0.833
h.	1:8	1/8	12.5%	0.125
i.	8:9	8/9	88.9%	0.889
j.	4:9	4/9	44.4%	0.444
k.	6:7	6/7	85.7%	0.857
l.	1:2	1/2	50%	0.5
m.	2:9	2/9	22.2%	0.222

Page 79:   Ratio Conversions

1102.

	Ratio	Fraction	Percent	Decimal
a.	8:9	8/9	88.9%	0.889
b.	4:4	4/4	100%	1
c.	3:8	3/8	37.5%	0.375
d.	2:7	2/7	28.6%	0.286
e.	1:10	1/10	10%	0.1
f.	1:6	1/6	16.7%	0.167
g.	7:10	7/10	70%	0.7
h.	1:5	1/5	20%	0.2
i.	2:4	2/4	50%	0.5
j.	4:6	4/6	66.7%	0.667
k.	4:7	4/7	57.1%	0.571
l.	2:6	2/6	33.3%	0.333
m.	4:5	4/5	80%	0.8

Page 80:   Cartesian Coordinates

1103.

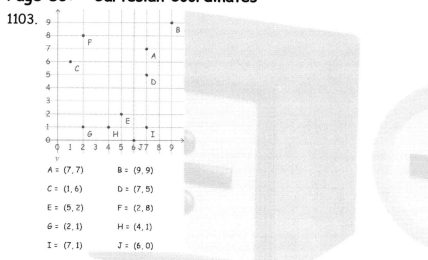

A = (7,7)   B = (9,9)

C = (1,6)   D = (7,5)

E = (5,2)   F = (2,8)

G = (2,1)   H = (4,1)

I = (7,1)   J = (6,0)

Page 81:   Cartesian Coordinates

1104.

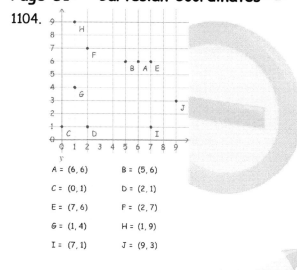

A = (6,6)   B = (5,6)

C = (0,1)   D = (2,1)

E = (7,6)   F = (2,7)

G = (1,4)   H = (1,9)

I = (7,1)   J = (9,3)

Page 82: Cartesian Coordinates

1105.

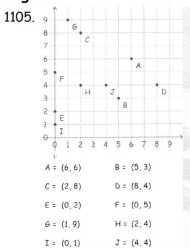

A = (6, 6)   B = (5, 3)

C = (2, 8)   D = (8, 4)

E = (0, 2)   F = (0, 5)

G = (1, 9)   H = (2, 4)

I = (0, 1)   J = (4, 4)

Page 83: Cartesian Coordinates

1106.

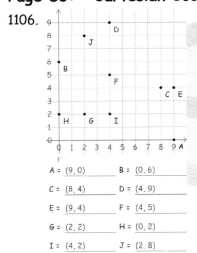

A = (9, 0)   B = (0, 6)

C = (8, 4)   D = (4, 9)

E = (9, 4)   F = (4, 5)

G = (2, 2)   H = (0, 2)

I = (4, 2)   J = (2, 8)

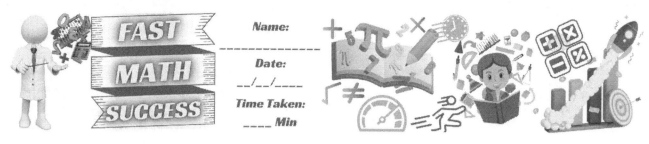
Page 84: Cartesian Coordinates

1107.

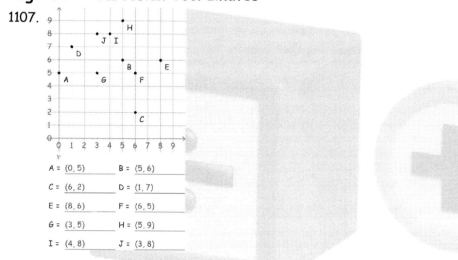

A = (0, 5)   B = (5, 6)

C = (6, 2)   D = (1, 7)

E = (8, 6)   F = (6, 5)

G = (3, 5)   H = (5, 9)

I = (4, 8)   J = (3, 8)

Page 85: Cartesian Coordinates

1108.

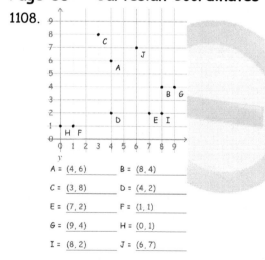

A = (4, 6)   B = (8, 4)

C = (3, 8)   D = (4, 2)

E = (7, 2)   F = (1, 1)

G = (9, 4)   H = (0, 1)

I = (8, 2)   J = (6, 7)

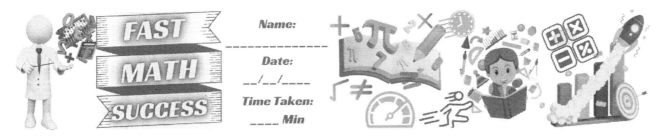

Page 86:   Cartesian Coordinates With Four Quadrants

1109.

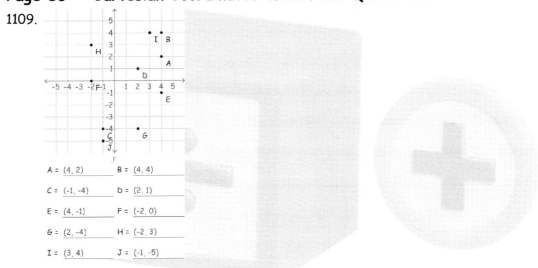

A = (4, 2)   B = (4, 4)

C = (-1, -4)   D = (2, 1)

E = (4, -1)   F = (-2, 0)

G = (2, -4)   H = (-2, 3)

I = (3, 4)   J = (-1, -5)

Page 87:   Cartesian Coordinates With Four Quadrants

1110.

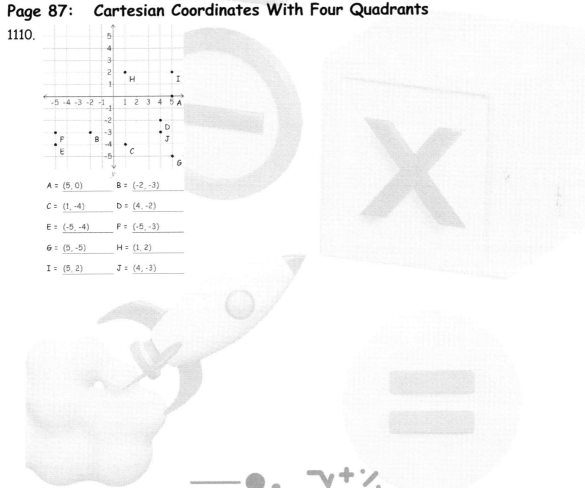

A = (5, 0)   B = (-2, -3)

C = (1, -4)   D = (4, -2)

E = (-5, -4)   F = (-5, -3)

G = (5, -5)   H = (1, 2)

I = (5, 2)   J = (4, -3)

Page 88: Cartesian Coordinates With Four Quadrants

1111.

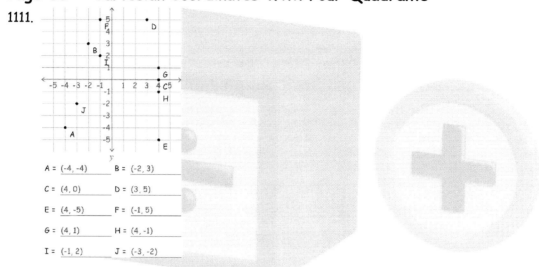

A = (-4, -4)	B = (-2, 3)
C = (4, 0)	D = (3, 5)
E = (4, -5)	F = (-1, 5)
G = (4, 1)	H = (4, -1)
I = (-1, 2)	J = (-3, -2)

Page 89: Cartesian Coordinates With Four Quadrants

1112.

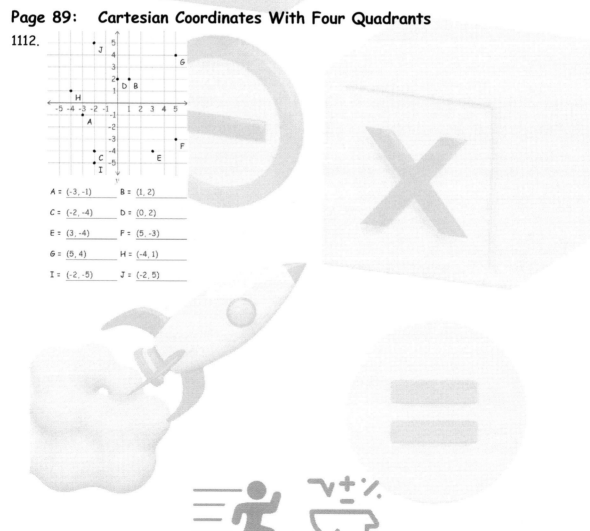

A = (-3, -1)	B = (1, 2)
C = (-2, -4)	D = (0, 2)
E = (3, -4)	F = (5, -3)
G = (5, 4)	H = (-4, 1)
I = (-2, -5)	J = (-2, 5)

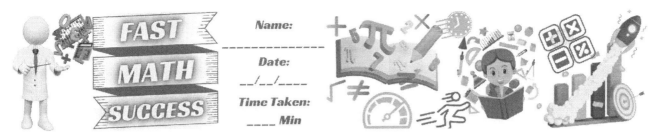

Page 90: Cartesian Coordinates With Four Quadrants

1113.

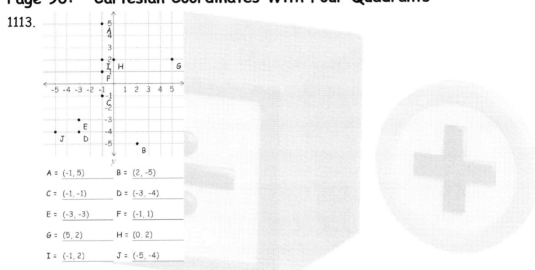

A = (-1, 5)	B = (2, -5)
C = (-1, -1)	D = (-3, -4)
E = (-3, -3)	F = (-1, 1)
G = (5, 2)	H = (0, 2)
I = (-1, 2)	J = (-5, -4)

Page 91: Cartesian Coordinates With Four Quadrants

1114.

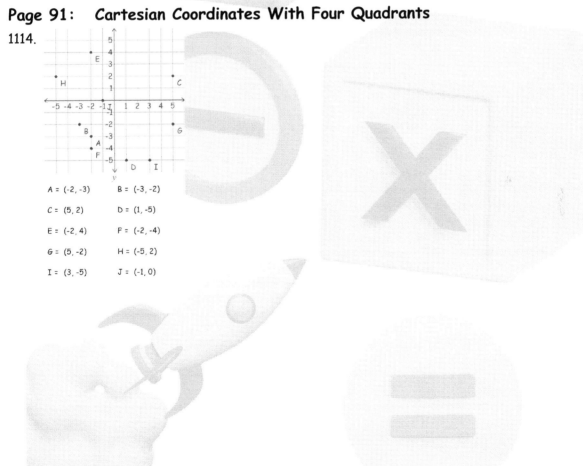

A = (-2, -3)	B = (-3, -2)
C = (5, 2)	D = (1, -5)
E = (-2, 4)	F = (-2, -4)
G = (5, -2)	H = (-5, 2)
I = (3, -5)	J = (-1, 0)

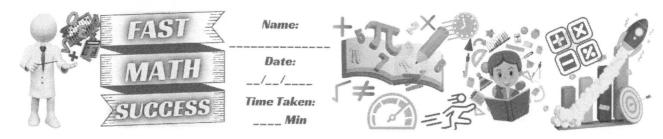

Page 92: Cartesian Coordinates With Four Quadrants

1115.

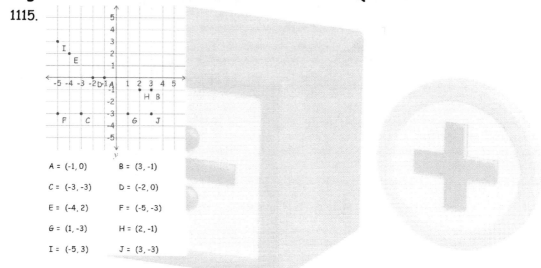

A = (-1, 0)	B = (3, -1)
C = (-3, -3)	D = (-2, 0)
E = (-4, 2)	F = (-5, -3)
G = (1, -3)	H = (2, -1)
I = (-5, 3)	J = (3, -3)

Page 93: Cartesian Coordinates With Four Quadrants

1116.

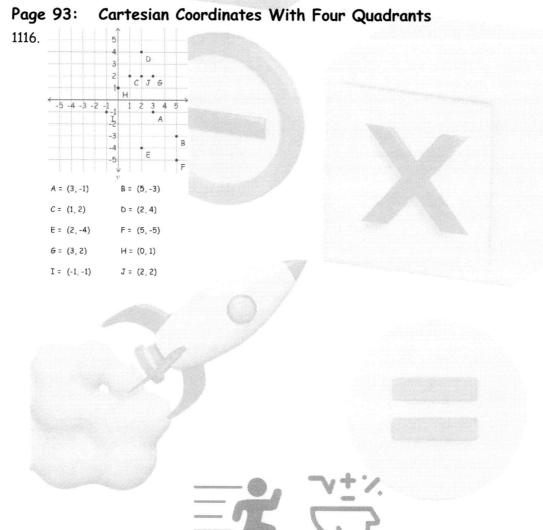

A = (3, -1)	B = (5, -3)
C = (1, 2)	D = (2, 4)
E = (2, -4)	F = (5, -5)
G = (3, 2)	H = (0, 1)
I = (-1, -1)	J = (2, 2)

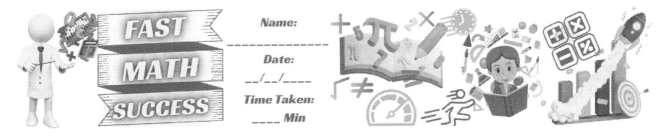
Page 94: Cartesian Coordinates With Four Quadrants

1117.

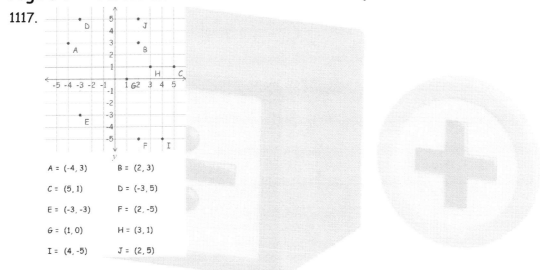

A = (-4, 3)	B = (2, 3)
C = (5, 1)	D = (-3, 5)
E = (-3, -3)	F = (2, -5)
G = (1, 0)	H = (3, 1)
I = (4, -5)	J = (2, 5)

Page 95: Cartesian Coordinates With Four Quadrants

1118.

A = (0, 3)	B = (0, 5)
C = (4, 0)	D = (-2, -1)
E = (2, -3)	F = (-5, 4)
G = (5, 4)	H = (4, -5)
I = (5, 5)	J = (3, 0)

Page 96: Plot Lines

1119.

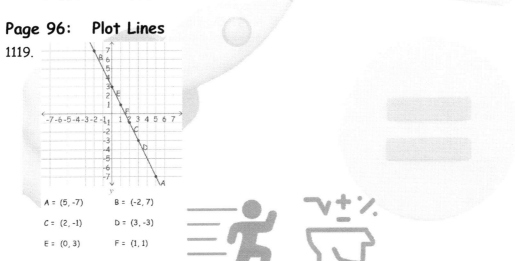

A = (5, -7)	B = (-2, 7)
C = (2, -1)	D = (3, -3)
E = (0, 3)	F = (1, 1)

Page 97:   Plot Lines

1120.

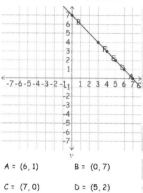

A = (6, 1)   B = (0, 7)

C = (7, 0)   D = (5, 2)

E = (4, 3)   F = (3, 4)

Page 98:   Plot Lines

1121.

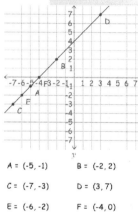

A = (-5, -1)   B = (-2, 2)

C = (-7, -3)   D = (3, 7)

E = (-6, -2)   F = (-4, 0)

Page 99:   Plot Lines

1122.

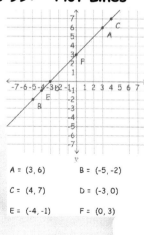

A = (3, 6)   B = (-5, -2)

C = (4, 7)   D = (-3, 0)

E = (-4, -1)   F = (0, 3)

Fast Math Success Workbook Grade 5-6

184

Page 100:   Plot Lines

1123.

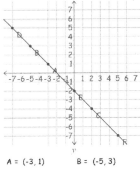

A = (-3, 1)   B = (-5, 3)

C = (2, -4)   D = (-7, 5)

E = (0, -2)   F = (5, -7)

Page 101:   Plot Lines

1124.

A = (4, 6)   B = (-3, 6)

C = (2, 6)   D = (3, 6)

E = (0, 6)   F = (-4, 6)

Page 102:   Plot Lines

1125.

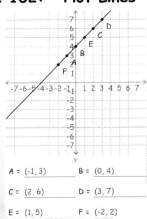

A = (-1, 3)   B = (0, 4)

C = (2, 6)   D = (3, 7)

E = (1, 5)   F = (-2, 2)

Page 103:   Plot Lines

1126.

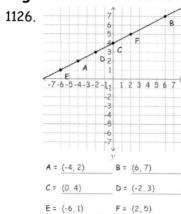

A = (-4, 2)   B = (6, 7)

C = (0, 4)   D = (-2, 3)

E = (-6, 1)   F = (2, 5)

Page 104:   Plot Lines

1127.

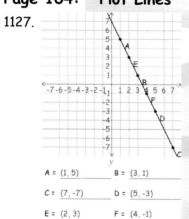

A = (1, 5)   B = (3, 1)

C = (7, -7)   D = (5, -3)

E = (2, 3)   F = (4, -1)

Page 105:   Plot Lines

1128.

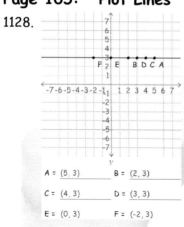

A = (5, 3)   B = (2, 3)

C = (4, 3)   D = (3, 3)

E = (0, 3)   F = (-2, 3)

Page 106:   Exponents

1129. **27,000**   1130. **7,225**   1131. **216**   1132. **54,872**

Name:

Date:
__/__/____

Time Taken:
____ Min

1133. **576**	1134. **205,379**	1135. **592,704**	1136. **493,039**
1137. **59,319**	1138. **1,156**	1139. **551,368**	1140. **681,472**
1141. **35,937**	1142. **8,281**	1143. **13,824**	1144. **324**
1145. **343**	1146. **373,248**	1147. **9,604**	1148. **7,569**

Page 107:   Exponents

1149. **54,872**	1150. **81**	1151. **3,844**	1152. **4,096**
1153. **144**	1154. **5,776**	1155. **1,521**	1156. **8,464**
1157. **2,704**	1158. **8**	1159. **32,768**	1160. **2,809**
1161. **2,500**	1162. **1,444**	1163. **3,721**	1164. **441**
1165. **389,017**	1166. **27**	1167. **592,704**	1168. **405,224**

Page 108:   Exponents

1169. **1,331**	1170. **784**	1171. **140,608**	1172. **195,112**
1173. **7,396**	1174. **405,224**	1175. **571,787**	1176. **39,304**
1177. **400**	1178. **3,969**	1179. **225**	1180. **4,225**
1181. **8,464**	1182. **4,096**	1183. **343,000**	1184. **5,041**
1185. **1,936**	1186. **8,281**	1187. **5,832**	1188. **884,736**

Page 109:   Exponents

1189. **24,389**	1190. **226,981**	1191. **27,000**	1192. **676**
1193. **17,576**	1194. **2,601**	1195. **3,481**	1196. **857,375**
1197. **1**	1198. **4,225**	1199. **140,608**	1200. **300,763**
1201. **2,916**	1202. **6,561**	1203. **961**	1204. **12,167**
1205. **68,921**	1206. **1,156**	1207. **7,921**	1208. **7,056**

Page 110:   Exponents

1209. **157,464**	1210. **216**	1211. **166,375**	1212. **970,299**
1213. **5,329**	1214. **5,625**	1215. **36**	1216. **2,197**
1217. **4,489**	1218. **91,125**	1219. **941,192**	1220. **3,721**

Fast Math Success Workbook Grade 5-6

Name:

Date:

__/__/____

Time Taken:

_____ Min

1221. **658,503**   1222. **1,000**   1223. **125**   1224. **1,936**

1225. **64**   1226. **42,875**   1227. **3,969**   1228. **1,089**

Page 111:   Scientific Notation

1229. **7.608 × 10^6**   1230. **5.733 × 10^6**   1231. **9.9 × 10^6**

1232. **6.6 × 10^6**   1233. **8.5 × 10^6**   1234. **9.141 × 10^6**

1235. **2.6 × 10^5**   1236. **5.74 × 10^6**   1237. **5.712 × 10^6**

1238. **7.31 × 10^6**   1239. **9.07 × 10^6**   1240. **3.674 × 10^6**

1241. **4.533 × 10^6**   1242. **5.826 × 10^6**   1243. **8.42 × 10^6**

1244. **6.429 × 10^6**   1245. **1.2 × 10^6**   1246. **2.988 × 10^6**

1247. **4.197 × 10^6**   1248. **7.6 × 10^6**

Page 112:   Scientific Notation

1249. **4.63 × 10^6**   1250. **6.006 × 10^6**   1251. **6.9 × 10^6**

1252. **6.94 × 10^5**   1253. **8.68 × 10^6**   1254. **7.7 × 10^6**

1255. **9 × 10^6**   1256. **4.2 × 10^6**   1257. **3.02 × 10^6**

1258. **4.6 × 10^6**   1259. **5.007 × 10^6**   1260. **1.8 × 10^6**

1261. **6.011 × 10^6**   1262. **6.595 × 10^6**   1263. **9.081 × 10^6**

1264. **7.96 × 10^5**   1265. **9.632 × 10^6**   1266. **1.9 × 10^6**

1267. **8.73 × 10^6**   1268. **2.12 × 10^6**

Page 113:   Scientific Notation

1269. **7.778 × 10^6**   1270. **1.2 × 10^6**   1271. **8.83 × 10^6**

1272. **5.86 × 10^5**   1273. **7.8 × 10^6**   1274. **5.745 × 10^6**

1275. **3.43 × 10^6**   1276. **4.746 × 10^6**   1277. **4.52 × 10^6**

1278. **1.357 × 10^6**   1279. **4.3 × 10^6**   1280. **9.2 × 10^6**

1281. **4.5 × 10^6**   1282. **5 × 10^5**   1283. **1.3 × 10^6**

1284. **4.137 × 10^6**   1285. **3.651 × 10^6**   1286. **5.424 × 10^6**

1287. **3.053 × 10^6**   1288. **8.938 × 10^6**

Fast Math Success Workbook Grade 5-6   **188**

Page 114:   Scientific Notation

1289. 251,000   1290. 1,200,000   1291. 4,190,000   1292. 2,810,000

1293. 8,130,000   1294. 4,940,000   1295. 9,280,000   1296. 8,206,000

1297. 8,478,000   1298. 5,796,000   1299. 6,670,000   1300. 5,981,000

1301. 3,000,000   1302. 2,518,000   1303. 2,510,000   1304. 1,000,000

1305. 8,480,000   1306. 2,200,000   1307. 470,000   1308. 5,976,000

Page 115:   Scientific Notation

1309. 8,657,000   1310. 3,428,000   1311. 1,770,000   1312. 1,758,000

1313. 9,320,000   1314. 350,000   1315. 3,918,000   1316. 1,930,000

1317. 2,900,000   1318. 230,000   1319. 943,000   1320. 1,400,000

1321. 3,500,000   1322. 6,210,000   1323. 2,936,000   1324. 9,087,000

1325. 2,688,000   1326. 459,000   1327. 7,200,000   1328. 630,000

Page 116:   Scientific Notation

1329. 7,880,000   1330. 5,331,000   1331. 7,723,000   1332. 3,776,000

1333. 7,324,000   1334. 1,080,000   1335. 6,000,000   1336. 5,800,000

1337. 5,983,000   1338. 3,608,000   1339. 5,400,000   1340. 6,700,000

1341. 1,690,000   1342. 9,300,000   1343. 1,010,000   1344. 4,949,000

1345. 1,171,000   1346. 7,700,000   1347. 7,115,000   1348. 5,582,000

Page 117:   Expressions - Single Step

1349. 9   1350. 5   1351. 1   1352. 8   1353. 2   1354. 7   1355. 8   1356. 7   1357. 5

1358. 5   1359. 6   1360. 9   1361. 6   1362. 2   1363. 2   1364. 8   1365. 4   1366. 4

1367. 8   1368. 9

Page 118:   Expressions - Single Step

1369. 3   1370. 6   1371. 1   1372. 3   1373. 8   1374. 2   1375. 8   1376. 7   1377. 4

1378. 6   1379. 9   1380. 8   1381. 1   1382. 1   1383. 8   1384. 1   1385. 3   1386. 8

1387. 7   1388. 7

Date:

__/__/____

Time Taken:

_____ Min

Page 119:   Expressions - Single Step

1389. **5**   1390. **9**   1391. **8**   1392. **5**   1393. **1**   1394. **5**   1395. **9**   1396. **5**   1397. **3**

1398. **3**   1399. **4**   1400. **9**   1401. **9**   1402. **7**   1403. **2**   1404. **6**   1405. **4**   1406. **4**

1407. **4**   1408. **6**

Page 120:   Expressions - Single Step

1409. **8**   1410. **6**   1411. **1**   1412. **2**   1413. **5**   1414. **9**   1415. **1**   1416. **8**   1417. **4**

1418. **5**   1419. **3**   1420. **3**   1421. **8**   1422. **8**   1423. **8**   1424. **1**   1425. **1**   1426. **4**

1427. **6**   1428. **3**

Page 121:   Expressions - Single Step

1429. **4**   1430. **9**   1431. **7**   1432. **6**   1433. **7**   1434. **3**   1435. **3**   1436. **9**   1437. **7**

1438. **3**   1439. **2**   1440. **3**   1441. **8**   1442. **7**   1443. **2**   1444. **2**   1445. **9**   1446. **2**

1447. **4**   1448. **9**

Page 122:   Number Problems

1449. **34**   1450. **16**   1451. **21**   1452. **8**   1453. **27**   1454. **20**   1455. **9**

1456. **10**   1457. **8**   1458. **45**

Page 123:   Number Problems

1459. **15**   1460. **24**   1461. **10**   1462. **3**   1463. **2**   1464. **11**   1465. **11**

1466. **5**   1467. **6**   1468. **28**

Page 124:   Number Problems

1469. **30**   1470. **2**   1471. **15**   1472. **4**   1473. **24**   1474. **19**   1475. **3**

1476. **26**   1477. **38**   1478. **32**

Page 125:   Number Problems

1479. **60**   1480. **16**   1481. **32**   1482. **11**   1483. **5**   1484. **22**   1485. **44**

1486. **13**   1487. **9**   1488. **45**

Page 126:   Number Problems

1489. **18**   1490. **46**   1491. **15**   1492. **30**   1493. **10**   1494. **37**   1495. **20**

1496. **19**   1497. **8**   1498. **17**

Fast Math Success Workbook Grade 5-6

Page 127: Pre-Algebra Equations (One Step) Addition and Subtraction

1499. x = 9	1500. x = 4	1501. x = 5	1502. x = 8	1503. x = 8
1504. x = 4	1505. x = 7	1506. x = 4	1507. x = 4	1508. x = 8
1509. x = 3	1510. x = 9	1511. x = 6	1512. x = 3	1513. x = 2
1514. x = 8	1515. x = 1	1516. x = 3	1517. x = 9	1518. x = 3

Page 128: Pre-Algebra Equations (One Step) Addition and Subtraction

1519. x = 2	1520. x = 4	1521. x = 9	1522. x = 1	1523. x = 5
1524. x = 8	1525. x = 6	1526. x = 1	1527. x = 3	1528. x = 2
1529. x = 4	1530. x = 9	1531. x = 6	1532. x = 2	1533. x = 9
1534. x = 2	1535. x = 2	1536. x = 3	1537. x = 4	1538. x = 8

Page 129: Pre-Algebra Equations (One Step) Addition and Subtraction

1539. x = 1	1540. x = 4	1541. x = 4	1542. x = 6	1543. x = 7
1544. x = 4	1545. x = 3	1546. x = 7	1547. x = 5	1548. x = 8
1549. x = 2	1550. x = 3	1551. x = 1	1552. x = 9	1553. x = 8
1554. x = 2	1555. x = 7	1556. x = 5	1557. x = 3	1558. x = 9

Page 130: Pre-Algebra Equations (One Step) Addition and Subtraction

1559. x = 2	1560. x = 9	1561. x = 7	1562. x = 1	1563. x = 5
1564. x = 7	1565. x = 8	1566. x = 7	1567. x = 2	1568. x = 8
1569. x = 9	1570. x = 3	1571. x = 6	1572. x = 6	1573. x = 5
1574. x = 8	1575. x = 9	1576. x = 4	1577. x = 9	1578. x = 4

Page 131: Pre-Algebra Equations (One Step) Addition and Subtraction

1579. x = 1	1580. x = 8	1581. x = 7	1582. x = 9	1583. x = 4
1584. x = 8	1585. x = 2	1586. x = 2	1587. x = 9	1588. x = 6
1589. x = 7	1590. x = 6	1591. x = 4	1592. x = 5	1593. x = 8
1594. x = 3	1595. x = 4	1596. x = 3	1597. x = 4	1598. x = 2

Name:
Date: __/__/____
Time Taken: ____ Min

Page 132:   Pre-Algebra Equations (One Step) Multiplication and Division

1599. x = 12	1600. x = 3	1601. x = 7	1602. x = 1	1603. x = 1
1604. x = 5	1605. x = 4	1606. x = 25	1607. x = 4	1608. x = 5
1609. x = 1	1610. x = 9	1611. x = 3	1612. x = 8	1613. x = 9
1614. x = 2	1615. x = 4	1616. x = 7	1617. x = 7	1618. x = 3

Page 133:   Pre-Algebra Equations (One Step) Multiplication and Division

1619. x = 18	1620. x = 8	1621. x = 7	1622. x = 2	1623. x = 1
1624. x = 2	1625. x = 2	1626. x = 3	1627. x = 5	1628. x = 2
1629. x = 6	1630. x = 6	1631. x = 2	1632. x = 6	1633. x = 6
1634. x = 1	1635. x = 2	1636. x = 3	1637. x = 9	1638. x = 7

Page 134:   Pre-Algebra Equations (One Step) Multiplication and Division

1639. x = 6	1640. x = 3	1641. x = 5	1642. x = 5	1643. x = 54
1644. x = 2	1645. x = 8	1646. x = 8	1647. x = 7	1648. x = 5
1649. x = 4	1650. x = 5	1651. x = 56	1652. x = 2	1653. x = 6
1654. x = 8	1655. x = 8	1656. x = 2	1657. x = 6	1658. x = 1

Page 135:   Pre-Algebra Equations (One Step) Multiplication and Division

1659. x = 9	1660. x = 9	1661. x = 8	1662. x = 4	1663. x = 7
1664. x = 3	1665. x = 7	1666. x = 6	1667. x = 35	1668. x = 2
1669. x = 2	1670. x = 9	1671. x = 5	1672. x = 4	1673. x = 1
1674. x = 2	1675. x = 4	1676. x = 8	1677. x = 1	1678. x = 1

Page 136:   Pre-Algebra Equations (One Step) Multiplication and Division

1679. x = 8	1680. x = 7	1681. x = 6	1682. x = 5	1683. x = 10
1684. x = 3	1685. x = 9	1686. x = 2	1687. x = 2	1688. x = 3
1689. x = 6	1690. x = 7	1691. x = 7	1692. x = 4	1693. x = 12
1694. x = 8	1695. x = 3	1696. x = 5	1697. x = 7	1698. x = 2

Name:

Date:

__/__/____

Time Taken:

____ Min

Page 137:   Inequalities - Addition and Subtraction

1699. x ≤ 7   1700. x < -3   1701. x > -6   1702. x < -3   1703. x ≤ -1

1704. x > 6

Page 138:   Inequalities - Addition and Subtraction

1705. x < 6   1706. x > 6   1707. x < -1   1708. x ≥ 1   1709. x ≤ 1

1710. x > 10

Page 139:   Inequalities - Addition and Subtraction

1711. x ≤ 15   1712. x ≤ 0   1713. x < 5   1714. x ≤ -1   1715. x > -2

1716. x ≤ 8

Page 140:   Inequalities - Multiplication and Division

1717. x < 1/3   1718. x ≥ 64   1719. x ≤ 2   1720. x ≤ 12   1721. x ≤ 2

1722. x < 12

Page 141:   Inequalities - Multiplication and Division

1723. x ≤ 4/3   1724. x ≥ 48   1725. x ≤ 3/4   1726. x < 6   1727. x < 48

1728. x > 3/5

Page 142:   Inequalities - Multiplication and Division

1729. x ≤ 4/5   1730. x ≤ 5   1731. x ≤ 12   1732. x > 1/3   1733. x ≤ 14

1734. x > 3/4

Page 143:   Find the Area and Perimeter

1735. P=43   A=78   1736. P=27   A=32   1737. P=34   A=35

1738. P=42   A=63   1739. P=34   A=60   1740. P=33   A=52.39

Page 144:   Find the Area and Perimeter

1741. P=28   A=48   1742. P=31   A=36.4   1743. P=54   A=140

1744. P=32   A=63   1745. P=36   A=62.35   1746. P=46   A=90

Page 145:   Find the Area and Perimeter

1747. P=60   A=188   1748. P=42   A=82.5   1749. P=34   A=48

1750. P=64   A=255   1751. P=40   A=99   1752. P=30   A=40

Page 146:   Find the Volume and Surface Area

1753. V=176.71 cm³ cm³ SA=181 cm² cm²

1754. V=12 cm³ cm³ SA=32 cm² cm²

1755. V=502.65 cm³ cm³ SA=352 cm² cm²

1756. V=80 cm³ cm³ SA=112 cm² cm²

1757. V=117 cm³ cm³ SA=152 cm² cm²

1758. V=26 cm³ cm³ SA=57 cm² cm²

Page 147:   Find the Volume and Surface Area

1759. V=252 cm³ cm³ SA=240 cm² cm²

1760. V=168 cm³ cm³ SA=188 cm² cm²

1761. V=220 cm³ cm³ SA=264.1 cm² cm²

1762. V=402.12 cm³ cm³ SA=302 cm² cm²

1763. V=117.81 cm³ cm³ SA=134 cm² cm²

1764. V=175 cm³ cm³ SA=190 cm² cm²

Page 148:   Find the Volume and Surface Area

1765. V=84 cm³ cm³ SA=135.4 cm² cm²

1766. V=140 cm³ cm³ SA=196.8 cm² cm²

1767. V=8 cm³ cm³ SA=24 cm² cm²

1768. V=84 cm³ cm³ SA=131 cm² cm²

1769. V=495 cm³ cm³ SA=426.6 cm² cm²

1770. V=34 cm³ cm³ SA=50 cm² cm²

Page 149:   Calculate the area of each circle.

1771. A=706.50 cm²   1772. A=3.14 cm²   1773. A=113.04 cm²

1774. A=452.16 cm²   1775. A=615.44 cm²   1776. A=803.84 cm²

Page 150:   Calculate the area of each circle.

1777. A=907.46 cm²   1778. A=1,133.54 cm²   1779. A=113.04 cm²

1780. A=78.50 cm²   1781. A=50.24 cm²   1782. A=12.56 cm²

Page 151: Calculate the area of each circle.

1783. A=1,256.00 cm²   1784. A=50.24 cm²   1785. A=452.16 cm²

1786. A=314.00 cm²   1787. A=803.84 cm²   1788. A=1,017.36 cm²

Page 152: Calculate the circumference of each circle.

1789. C=100.48 cm   1790. C=75.36 cm   1791. C=69.08 cm

1792. C=94.20 cm   1793. C=113.04 cm   1794. C=6.28 cm

Page 153: Calculate the circumference of each circle.

1795. C=43.96 cm   1796. C=25.12 cm   1797. C=106.76 cm

1798. C=6.28 cm   1799. C=125.60 cm   1800. C=100.48 cm

Page 154: Calculate the circumference of each circle.

1801. C=113.04 cm   1802. C=62.80 cm   1803. C=12.56 cm

1804. C=75.36 cm   1805. C=81.64 cm   1806. C=119.32 cm

Page 155: Measure of Center - Mean

1807. Mean = 39.75   1808. Mean = 50.333   1809. Mean = 43.444

1810. Mean = 47   1811. Mean = 58.444   1812. Mean = 67.5

Page 156: Measure of Center - Mean

1813. Mean = 42.375   1814. Mean = 56.889   1815. Mean = 42.5

1816. Mean = 43   1817. Mean = 54   1818. Mean = 49.778

Page 157: Measure of Center - Median

1819. Median = 37   1820. Median = 23.5   1821. Median = 43.5

1822. Median = 63   1823. Median = 52   1824. Median = 30.5

Page 158: Measure of Center - Median

1825. Median = 49   1826. Median = 36   1827. Median = 45.5

1828. Median = 40   1829. Median = 49   1830. Median = 60

Page 159: Measure of Center - Mode

1831. Mode = none   1832. Mode = 25   1833. Mode = 90

1834. **Mode** = none   1835. **Mode** = none   1836. **Mode** = 33

Page 160:   **Measure of Center - Mode**

1837. **Mode** = 98   1838. **Mode** = 98   1839. **Mode** = none

1840. **Mode** = none   1841. **Mode** = 88   1842. **Mode** = none

Page 161:   **Measure of Variability - Range**

1843. **Range** = 65   1844. **Range** = 62   1845. **Range** = 74   1846. **Range** = 92

1847. **Range** = 88   1848. **Range** = 92

Page 162:   **Measure of Variability - Range**

1849. **Range** = 55   1850. **Range** = 85   1851. **Range** = 51   1852. **Range** = 94

1853. **Range** = 64   1854. **Range** = 91

Made in the USA
Las Vegas, NV
09 January 2024